Introduction to AI Agents: Concepts, Types, and Applications

Kaelix Draven

Let me tell you a story.

It all began one late night, somewhere between a second cup of coffee and my fifteenth browser tab open to obscure AI forums, when I asked myself a question that would change everything: What in the world is an AI agent? I mean, I'd heard the term tossed around like digital confetti—autonomous agents, intelligent agents, goal-driven agents, agents with attitudes. But what was one, really? A glorified chatbot? A Roomba with ambition? A cyber-butler waiting for its big break?

That question didn't just pull me into the rabbit hole—it flung me down headfirst. And now, after years of study, experimentation, occasional panic, and more caffeine than is medically advisable, you're holding the result: **Introduction to AI Agents: Concepts, Types, and Applications**. This book is the starting line in a ten-part series called *Mastering AI Agents: From Theory to Deployment*. Think of it as your backstage pass to the minds of the machines.

This series was born out of a simple but dangerous idea: What if I could break down the complex world of AI agents in a way that's not just digestible—but actually fun to read? No dry theory, no math-induced migraines. Just practical insights, exciting possibilities, and a touch of irreverent humor to keep things human. Because if we're going to spend the next few hundred pages talking about artificial intelligence, I figure we better not sound too artificial ourselves.

So what's in this book?

This first volume—your trusty AI Agent 101—is where we set the foundation. We'll start with the basics: what makes an agent an agent, how they interact with their environments, and why the word "rational" means something very specific (and sometimes very weird) in AI. We'll dissect sensors and actuators, talk about what an agent knows (and what it thinks it knows), and dive into the architectural madness of rule-based brains vs. learning-based minds.

You'll meet reflex agents who react faster than a squirrel on espresso, goal-based agents who chase outcomes like determined toddlers in a toy store, and utility-based agents who've practically got their own TED Talks on decision theory. Oh, and let's not forget the learning agents—those delightful bundles of digital curiosity who grow wiser every time they mess up.

By the time we hit Chapter 9, we'll start exploring how these agents are sneaking into your everyday life. From virtual assistants that pretend to understand you (bless their circuits), to smart homes, chatbots, and automated trading systems that never sleep, we're talking full invasion. And in the final chapter, I'll take you on a ride into the future, where ethics, collaboration, and trust take center stage. It's not all robots and rainbows—we'll wrestle with the tough questions too.

But this book is only the beginning. Like any good origin story, it sets the stage for what's to come. And what's coming next? Oh, just the rest of the Mastering AI Agents series, where we roll up our sleeves and start building, training, deploying, and (occasionally) debugging our way to greatness.

In the second book, **Building AI Agents with Python**, we'll get our hands dirty. It's code, code, glorious code—and I'll walk you through every keystroke. You don't have to be a Python wizard to keep up. Just bring curiosity and a keyboard.

Book three, **Reinforcement Learning for AI Agents**, is where things get wild. Agents that learn through trial and error, chasing rewards like a digital dopamine hit? Yes please. We'll talk Markov Decision Processes, Q-learning, and why failure is not only an option—it's a requirement.

In **Multi-Agent Systems**, things get complicated. Think of it as a digital sitcom: agents working together, competing, communicating, arguing over who gets access to the shared data. Hilarity (and complexity) ensues.

Then we hit the streets—**AI Agents in the Real World** takes everything we've learned and drops it into homes, factories, cities, and research labs. This is where the theory meets the thermostat.

Automation gets its own spotlight in **AI Agents for Automation**. We'll explore everything from chatbots with personality disorders to virtual assistants that are almost too helpful. (Seriously, Siri, I said "call Mom," not "call my boss.")

In **AI Agents in Finance**, it's Wall Street meets code. Whether it's spotting fraud faster than a human blink or executing trades while the rest of us are still sipping coffee, agents are rewriting the rulebook.

Then we lift off—literally—with **AI Agents for Robotics**. We'll explore smart drones, autonomous vehicles, and how agents learn to move through the real world without constantly bumping into things. (Unlike me on Monday mornings.)

In **AI Agents in Healthcare**, we look at the life-saving side of AI: diagnosis, treatment planning, and even drug discovery. Because when an agent can help detect cancer early, that's the kind of intelligence we want everywhere.

Finally, we wrap it all up with **AI Agents for Cybersecurity**, where we pit agents against digital villains. It's a high-stakes game of cat and mouse—and spoiler alert: the mice are very, very smart.

Now I know what you might be thinking: "That's a lot of books." And you're right. But here's the thing—I didn't write this series to impress the academic elite. I wrote it for you. For the coder, the tinkerer, the dreamer, the skeptic. For the college student trying to survive AI 101. For the startup founder pitching their next agent-powered app. For the curious human who just wants to know how machines think (or at least pretend to).

I'm not here to sell you on AI hype or peddle robotic utopias. I'm here to guide you through the real stuff—the architecture, the algorithms, the "aha!" moments, and the late-night bugs that don't make any sense until coffee kicks in.

So buckle up. Introduction to AI Agents is your boarding pass to a universe of digital minds, strange decisions, and smarter machines. It's going to be weird. It's going to be wonderful. And by the end, you'll not only understand AI agents—you might just want to build one of your own.

Welcome to the start of something incredible.

Let's get agent-y.

Chapter 1: Understanding AI Agents

If you've ever yelled at your voice assistant for misinterpreting "play jazz" as "call Jeff," you've already met an AI agent in the wild. They're the digital gremlins quietly running our smart homes, our apps, and—occasionally—our coffee machines. But what are these things, really? Are they intelligent? Are they aware? Can they be bribed with data cookies? This chapter kicks things off with the basics: what AI agents are, why they matter, and how they've evolved from rule-following bots into semi-autonomous digital lifeforms with suspiciously good timing.

Formally, this chapter introduces the foundational concept of an AI agent, its definition, and historical background. We explore how intelligent agents operate within environments through continuous interaction loops, and we define rationality and performance measures that guide agent behavior. Additionally, we examine different types of environments—observable, deterministic, episodic, and more—and how these influence agent design and decision-making.

1.1 What is an AI Agent?

Let's start with a confession. The first time I heard the term "AI agent," I imagined a sleek, sunglasses-wearing robot kicking down doors, saying things like "Objective acquired," and dramatically leaping out of helicopters. And while that's technically the plot of at least three science fiction movies, it's not quite what we mean in the world of artificial intelligence.

An AI agent, in the most un-glamorous but super-useful way possible, is an autonomous entity that perceives its environment and takes actions to achieve a specific goal. That's it. No sunglasses. No explosions. Just a system that observes, processes, and responds. But don't let the simplicity of that definition fool you—behind it lies a mountain of design decisions, algorithms, architectures, and headaches (the fun kind).

So, what exactly does it mean to "perceive" and "act"? Let's break it down.

Agents: Not Just for Spy Movies

At its core, an agent is anything that can take in information from its surroundings—what we call perception—and then do something based on that—what we call action. It could be as simple as a motion sensor light that turns on when you walk past (hello, reflex agent), or as complex as a Mars rover navigating alien terrain without constant instructions from Earth.

To qualify as an AI agent, though, it needs a little more than just reactivity. It needs autonomy, adaptability, and some degree of intelligence. That means it can make decisions based on its inputs without a human micromanaging every move. It might learn from its experiences, build internal models of the world, or weigh options based on expected outcomes. Fancy stuff.

Let's Talk Anatomy (Don't Worry, No Dissections)

Every AI agent has a few key components, kind of like a digital anatomy lesson:

Sensors – These are the agent's eyes and ears (sometimes metaphorical, sometimes literal). They collect data from the environment. For a robot, this could be cameras or LIDAR. For a chatbot, it might be user input from a keyboard.

Actuators – These are the limbs or tools the agent uses to affect its environment. Wheels, arms, software commands, emails—basically, how the agent "does stuff."

Agent Function – This is the secret sauce. It's the mathematical or logical function that maps from perceptions to actions. Think of it as the brain or the decision-making center.

Performance Measure – Every agent has a goal, whether it's to vacuum a room efficiently, answer customer queries, or win at chess. The performance measure is how we score it. It's the report card of agenthood.

An Example You've Already Met

Let's use an example you've probably encountered: a virtual assistant like Alexa or Siri. When you say, "What's the weather today?", your voice is picked up by a microphone (sensor). That input gets transformed into a digital signal, interpreted by a speech recognition model, and passed to the assistant's decision-making logic. It searches for the weather, finds a response, and replies through a speaker (actuator).

That entire flow—from hearing your voice to giving a spoken answer—was handled by an AI agent. And in most cases, it was done in less than a second. Which is impressive… unless it thought you said "play reggae" instead of "rain today."

Environment: The Agent's Playground

An agent doesn't exist in a vacuum (unless it's a literal robotic vacuum). It operates within an environment, and understanding this environment is crucial to designing a smart, effective agent.

Environments can be:

Fully Observable (the agent sees everything, like in chess) or Partially Observable (the agent only sees some things, like in poker).

Deterministic (same action = same result) or Stochastic (outcomes are probabilistic).

Static (the environment doesn't change while the agent thinks) or Dynamic (the world moves on, with or without the agent).

Episodic (decisions don't affect future ones) or Sequential (everything matters—like life).

The type of environment deeply influences how we design the agent. A simple reflex agent might survive in a static, fully observable world, but throw it into a dynamic, partially observable one, and it'll be as confused as a cat in a mirror maze.

Rationality: It's Not What You Think

Here's the twist: we don't define an intelligent agent by how human it seems. We define it by how rational it is.

A rational agent chooses actions that maximize its expected performance, given what it knows. It's not about being emotional or creative—it's about doing the best possible thing with the available data.

This is huge. It means even a really simple agent can be considered "intelligent" if it consistently makes good choices. And it also means that flashy, complicated behavior doesn't automatically mean smarter—just ask that chatbot that writes poems but can't schedule a meeting correctly.

So... Why Should I Care?

Because AI agents are everywhere. They're in your phone, your car, your fridge, your social media feed (sorry about that), your bank, your hospital, and maybe even your vacuum cleaner. The more you understand how they think and operate, the better positioned you are to build, improve, or just not be mystified by them.

Also, let's be honest: understanding AI agents is one of those superpowers that makes you sound extremely cool in conversation. Try casually dropping "bounded rationality" into your next group chat and watch the respect roll in.

But Wait, There's More…

This chapter is just the tip of the algorithmic iceberg. In the coming sections, we'll explore the evolution of intelligent agents (spoiler: they didn't start smart), dive into how agents interact with their environments over time, and unpack what it really means to perform well.

So if you're still imagining AI agents as little digital spies with trench coats and laser eyes—keep going. You're not entirely wrong. But by the end of this book, you'll see them for what they really are: data-driven, logic-fueled, environment-wrangling problem solvers. With just enough bugs to keep things interesting.

Now, if you'll excuse me, I need to go reboot an AI agent that recently declared itself the "King of Thermostats." Agents: always learning. Sometimes too much.

1.2 History and Evolution of Intelligent Agents

Before we dive deep, a small warning: history can be dry. Like, "mouthful of sawdust" dry. But not here, my friend. Buckle up, because the story of intelligent agents is a wild, nerdy ride filled with lofty dreams, shocking setbacks, and more optimism than a coffee-fueled college hackathon.

It all starts, as most great things do, with an impossible idea: Can we make a machine that thinks and acts intelligently?

The Birth of a Dream (1940s–1950s)

Once upon a time, in the dim, flickering light of post-WWII computer labs, a few pioneers dared to dream crazy dreams. Alan Turing (yes, that Turing) asked a deceptively simple question: "Can machines think?" His 1950 paper "Computing Machinery and Intelligence" didn't just ask—it challenged. It laid the groundwork for everything that came next.

Turing's famous "Imitation Game," now known as the Turing Test, became the first benchmark for machine intelligence. If a machine could carry on a conversation indistinguishable from a human's, it could be considered "intelligent." Notice, even here, the seeds of agents were being planted: interact with the environment (conversation) and respond appropriately (actions).

Meanwhile, the first actual attempts at building intelligent programs—early symbolic AI—began to sprout. These were systems that used rules and logic to solve problems, like playing chess or proving theorems. Programs like Logic Theorist (1956) and General Problem Solver (1957) were among the first that you could squint at and call "agents"—simple, rule-following entities trying to achieve a goal.

Spoiler alert: they were impressive… in a "baby's first steps" kind of way.

The Rise of Symbolic AI (1950s–1970s)

The early AI researchers were riding high. They thought human-level intelligence was just a few summers of coding away. (Bless their hearts.)

This era birthed the concept of expert systems—programs loaded with human knowledge that could make decisions in narrow fields like medicine (hello, MYCIN in the 1970s). These systems could be seen as early knowledge-based agents: they collected information, reasoned over it, and made decisions.

But here's the kicker: these agents were brittle. Change the environment even a little bit? Boom. Useless. They had no learning ability, no adaptability. Basically, they were really smart... until they weren't.

The AI Winter(s) (1970s–1990s)

Here comes the dramatic music: DUN DUN DUN.

Reality hit hard. Despite the hype, early agents couldn't deliver on the sky-high promises. Funding dried up. Public excitement fizzled. TWICE. We call these sad times the AI Winters—periods where saying "I work in AI" got you less of a "Wow!" and more of a sympathetic pat on the back.

But even in the cold, important seeds were being planted. Researchers started to realize that real intelligence wasn't just about crunching rules—it was about learning, adapting, perceiving, and surviving in complex environments.

This set the stage for the next revolution.

The Rise of Learning Agents (1990s–2000s)

Enter machine learning—where instead of telling the agent every possible rule, we let it figure things out from experience.

This was HUGE. Suddenly, agents didn't have to know everything from the start. They could explore, learn, and even recover from mistakes (unlike my poor Roomba that once tried to eat a sock and gave up on life).

Reinforcement learning became a hot area: agents learned what actions led to rewards and punishments. The classic example? Teaching an AI to play games like chess or Go— and eventually watching it defeat human world champions in spectacular, humbling fashion.

Multi-agent systems also started gaining attention. Instead of just one agent doing its thing, researchers explored how multiple agents could cooperate (or compete) to solve problems. Think robot teams, swarm drones, or even virtual economies.

The Modern Era (2010s–Today)

Today, intelligent agents are everywhere, often hidden in plain sight. Your smartphone? It's packed with them. Recommendation engines, autonomous cars, industrial robots, personalized healthcare advisors—you name it.

Thanks to deep learning and massive data, modern agents can perceive the world through computer vision, natural language processing, and other superpowers. They can adapt faster, plan better, and (sometimes) even explain themselves.

But we're still facing big challenges:

How do we make agents transparent and explainable?

How do we handle ethics when agents make decisions that affect human lives?

How do we ensure agents remain aligned with human goals, even as they become smarter?

In short: we've come a long way from the 1950s dreamers—but the journey is far from over.

From Logic Choppers to Learning Explorers

Looking back, it's almost funny how confident early AI pioneers were. But honestly? Their ambition lit the fire that powers everything we do today. Without their wild dreams—and spectacular failures—we wouldn't have the sophisticated, adaptive agents that we now rely on every day.

Agents have evolved from simple, rule-following logic bots into complex, environment-savvy decision-makers. They've gone from chessboards to real-world chaos, and they're just getting started.

And if history teaches us anything, it's this: underestimating the future of AI agents is like underestimating a cat with access to a laser pointer. Things are going to get very interesting, very fast.

Now, if you'll excuse me, I'm off to check on my personal assistant AI—it recently started recommending I wear "wizard robes" for meetings. Progress, people. Progress.

1.3 The Agent-Environment Interaction Loop

Picture this: you're at a party. (Yes, AI engineers go to parties too, sometimes.) You walk into the room, take a quick look around, spot a table full of snacks, and make a beeline for the nachos. Congratulations—you've just participated in the Agent-Environment Interaction Loop.

Okay, maybe you didn't realize you were starring in a live demonstration of a core AI concept, but that's exactly what happened. You perceived your environment (snacks detected), made a decision (nachos over everything), and acted accordingly (nom nom nom).

This, my friend, is the very heart of how intelligent agents operate. Not the nachos part (sadly), but the loop—the continuous cycle of sensing, thinking, acting, and repeating. It's simple in theory but insanely powerful in practice. Let's dig in.

The Loop That Runs the World

At its core, the Agent-Environment Interaction Loop is the never-ending conversation between an agent and its surroundings. It goes a little something like this:

Perceive: The agent collects data from the environment through its sensors.

Decide: Based on the current perception and its internal goals or knowledge, the agent decides what to do.

Act: The agent executes an action that affects the environment.

Repeat: Because the environment might change, the agent goes back to Step 1. Endlessly.

And there you have it. The entire basis of intelligent behavior, distilled into four glorious, caffeine-fueled steps.

A More Serious (but Still Fun) Example

Imagine a self-driving car (one of the flashiest agents out there). Here's its loop:

Perceive: Sensors pick up lane markings, nearby vehicles, pedestrians, and traffic lights.

Decide: Based on traffic laws, safety protocols, and navigation goals, the car decides to slow down because a pedestrian is crossing.

Act: It applies the brakes.

Repeat: After stopping, it reassesses the environment and decides when it's safe to move again.

This loop needs to happen hundreds, even thousands of times per second. If the car blinked and missed a second of updates, the result could be... well, less "cool AI innovation" and more "insurance nightmare."

Why the Loop Matters

You might be wondering, "Kaelix, why are you hammering this loop thing so hard?"

Because this loop is what separates an intelligent agent from a static program.

A normal program might follow a straight line: input → output → done.

An agent? It lives inside the loop. It's always listening, always updating, always acting. It doesn't just react; it interacts. And if it's a really clever agent, it even plans ahead for future perceptions and actions.

Without the loop, agents would be like wind-up toys—cute for five seconds, then useless. With the loop, they can operate in messy, unpredictable real-world environments, adapting as they go.

Sensors, Actions, and Feedback, Oh My

Let's take a slightly closer look at the ingredients:

Sensors: These aren't always physical gadgets. For a chess-playing AI, the "sensor" could be the digital game board. For a chatbot, it's the text input. The important thing is that the agent has a way to "feel" the environment.

Actuators: Again, this doesn't have to mean robot arms (though robot arms are objectively cool). For a software agent, "actuators" might be sending a message, moving a game piece, or updating a database.

Feedback Loop: Actions change the environment, which means the next perception is different. The agent learns whether its actions brought it closer to its goals or pushed it further away. It's like playing a game of hot-and-cold with the universe.

This feedback is how agents get smarter over time. They notice patterns. They refine strategies. They don't just memorize—they evolve.

Environment Isn't Always Fair

Here's the kicker: the environment doesn't always play nice.

Sometimes it's stochastic (random stuff happens).

Sometimes it's partially observable (you can't see everything you need to).

Sometimes it's dynamic (the situation keeps changing even while you think).

Sometimes it's just downright hostile (looking at you, cybersecurity threats).

This is why building good agents is an art as much as a science. They have to deal with uncertainty, incomplete information, unexpected obstacles, and those deeply frustrating moments when nothing behaves the way it's supposed to. (Kind of like parenting.)

Reflex Agents vs. Learning Agents

Not all agents handle the loop the same way.

Simple Reflex Agents: They see and act immediately, based on fixed rules. ("If wall ahead ➜ turn left.") Great for quick responses but terrible at complex tasks.

Model-Based Agents: They build internal maps or models of the environment. They can reason about the unseen parts and plan better.

Learning Agents: The heavyweights. They analyze the outcomes of their actions and adjust future behavior. Each loop makes them smarter. They're basically the AI version of, "I learned from my mistakes" (except, you know, actually true).

The fancier the agent, the more sophisticated its use of the loop becomes.

A Loop with No End in Sight

Here's the beautiful—and slightly terrifying—part:

The Agent-Environment Interaction Loop is infinite.

As long as the agent is "alive" (powered, deployed, and relevant), it keeps cycling. It never really "finishes" because the environment is always evolving. Think about your Roomba— it doesn't clean your house once and say, "My job here is done." Nope. Every dust bunny, every Lego left out, every rearranged piece of furniture triggers a new loop.

And that's the magic. Intelligent agents aren't statues. They are dancers, moving rhythmically with the environment, one perception-action beat at a time.

If you take nothing else from this chapter, remember this:

Good agents think fast. Great agents loop faster.

And the best ones? They learn something new every spin around the dance floor.

Now if you'll excuse me, I need to go recalibrate my coffee-making robot. It's decided that "one sugar" means "dump the entire bag in." Agents: endlessly looping. Occasionally hyper-caffeinating.

1.4 Rationality and Performance Measures

Imagine hiring a personal assistant who, upon hearing you're late for a meeting, calmly hands you a sandwich instead of calling you a ride. Technically, they acted. They did something. But was it the right thing? Was it rational? In the world of AI agents, this is not just a funny story—it's a critical distinction.

Welcome to the world of rationality and performance measures, where we ask the most important questions in AI agent design: Is the agent making smart decisions? And how do we even measure that?

Hold onto your thinking caps. Things are about to get delightfully nerdy.

What Is Rationality, Anyway?

- Rationality, in AI agent land, doesn't mean "emotional coldness" or "calculator brain." It simply means:
- Choosing actions that are expected to maximize goal achievement, given the information available.

In simpler terms:

See the world (imperfectly).

Make the best decision you can.

Act to achieve your goals.

Notice the catch: agents don't have to be perfect. They just have to do the best they can with what they know. (Kind of like trying to find the bathroom in a restaurant you've never been to—you guess based on signs and smells, and hope for the best.)

This is called bounded rationality—making the smartest decision possible within the limits of available information, resources, and time.

Rational ≠ Omniscient

One of the biggest mistakes beginners make when designing AI agents? Expecting them to be omniscient. Newsflash: no agent (and no human) has perfect knowledge of their environment.

Rational agents operate under uncertainty all the time:

Is the road ahead icy?

Will the stock market crash tomorrow?

Will Kaelix's coffee machine launch a caffeine rebellion?

Given incomplete data, agents must still choose actions that are likely to lead to success. They don't sit there paralyzed, waiting for divine certainty. They act, based on the best guess at the time.

Sometimes they win. Sometimes they fail gloriously. Either way, rationality is about the quality of decision-making, not the outcome itself.

How Do We Know If an Agent Is Rational?

Here's where performance measures enter the stage like a boss battle mini-boss.

Performance measures are the yardsticks we use to judge whether an agent is doing its job well. They must be:

Objective (no wishy-washy "vibes" allowed)

Relevant to the agent's goals

Measurable in the real world

For a self-driving car, a performance measure might be:

Number of safe trips completed without accidents

Average time to destination

Fuel efficiency

For a chess-playing agent:

Number of games won

Average depth of search per move

For a coffee-fetching robot:

Number of coffee cups delivered unspilled

Number of employees now dependent on caffeine IV drips

The performance measure must reflect the actual goal, not just the agent's internal processes. Nobody cares how many database lookups the car did if it crashed into a tree.

Designing Good Performance Measures

Pro tip from someone who's been in the trenches:

Bad performance measures make bad agents.

If you reward an agent for the wrong things, you'll get hilarious, horrifying results. Classic examples include:

A cleaning robot rewarded for "spotless floors" simply covering dirt with carpet.

A game-playing AI rewarded for "high score" finding bugs in the code to earn infinite points.

An AI meant to "maximize user engagement" accidentally radicalizing its users for more clicks.

In short: be careful what you wish for. Agents are brutally literal. They will maximize whatever you tell them to... even if it leads to catastrophe.

Designing thoughtful, comprehensive performance measures is an art. It forces you to really think about what success looks like, and how it can be measured accurately without unintended side effects.

Rationality Over Time

Another important bit: rationality isn't judged at one frozen moment. Agents operate over time.

Good agents consider:

Immediate consequences

Long-term impacts

Trade-offs between short-term gains and long-term goals

This leads into fields like planning and deliberative reasoning, which we'll geek out about in later chapters. For now, just remember:

A truly rational agent is playing chess with reality, thinking several moves ahead, not just reacting to the now.

Rational Agents: Real-World Examples

Let's bring it down from the clouds:

Netflix's Recommendation Engine: Suggests shows based on what you're likely to watch. Rational? Mostly. Unless you count that weird night you ended up in a rabbit hole of Norwegian death metal documentaries.

Autonomous Drones: Navigate forests, find missing hikers, avoid obstacles. Rational? Very, assuming you trained them well.

Spam Filters: Identify and block junk emails. Rational? Absolutely. Unless they start blocking your mom's "forwarded chain letters" (which honestly, maybe isn't such a bad thing).

Each of these agents works with partial information, limited time, and evolving environments. Yet they manage to achieve their goals, optimizing performance measures we set for them.

In Summary (and Also, Maybe Your Life Motto)

A rational agent chooses the best action it can, based on what it knows, to achieve its goals as measured by clear, smart performance criteria.

Simple to say. Devilishly tricky to pull off.

And hey, if your agent makes a mistake? Remember: humans built it.
And we're the same species that once thought mullets were a good idea.

Rationality: the never-ending work in progress!

1.5 Types of Environments and Their Impact on Agents

Let's play a quick game: would you rather be a superhero saving the world in a calm, predictable town... or in a chaotic city where the laws of physics randomly change every Tuesday? If you chose the first option, congratulations—you understand the critical importance of an environment.

Now, apply that thinking to AI agents. An agent's environment can make or break its success, no matter how smart it is. You could design the most brilliant agent on Earth, but if you drop it into the wrong kind of environment without preparation, it'll be like trying to win a NASCAR race while riding a unicycle.

Today, we're diving into the different types of environments agents can face—and trust me, they're wilder than a raccoon in a vending machine.

Environment Basics: More Than Just "Out There"

First, a reality check: when we say "environment," we don't mean "trees and lakes" (although that could be one, too).
In AI, the environment is whatever the agent interacts with—the space where its sensors pick up information and its actuators make changes.

This could be:

A chess board

A messy human kitchen

The entire global internet

A Martian landscape full of dust storms

The type of environment dramatically affects the strategies and architectures an agent must use. So let's break these down into the classic categories.

Fully Observable vs. Partially Observable

Fully Observable: The agent's sensors can access the complete state of the environment at any given time. No hidden surprises.

Example: A chess board—every piece is visible to both players all the time.

Partially Observable: The agent only sees part of the environment at once. Hidden information, noise, or bad sensors might obscure key details.

Example: A self-driving car in heavy fog—good luck spotting that pedestrian crossing three lanes over.

Impact on Agents:

In fully observable environments, agents can plan with certainty. In partially observable ones, they must maintain belief states—educated guesses about the world's true condition. Suddenly, life gets trickier.

Deterministic vs. Stochastic

Deterministic: Every action has a predictable outcome. If you press a button, you know exactly what happens next.

Example: Moving a chess piece—the rook never randomly explodes (unless you're playing really creative house rules).

Stochastic: Actions have unpredictable results, often due to random elements or hidden variables.

Example: A delivery robot navigating traffic—maybe the light turns green, maybe someone jaywalks at the last second.

Impact on Agents:

Deterministic environments allow for "if X, then Y" programming. Stochastic environments require agents to plan probabilistically, handling risks and building in contingencies.

Episodic vs. Sequential

Episodic: Each experience (or task) is independent of previous ones. What happens now doesn't affect the future.

Example: Sorting packages in a warehouse—whether you placed box A correctly has no bearing on box B.

Sequential: Current decisions do affect future states and opportunities.

Example: In chess, one bad move now can haunt you for the rest of the game (or in my case, usually within five moves).

Impact on Agents:

Episodic environments allow for simpler decision-making. Sequential ones force agents to think long-term, managing consequences over multiple steps.

Static vs. Dynamic

Static: The environment stays the same unless the agent acts.

Example: A crossword puzzle doesn't fill itself in when you blink.

Dynamic: The environment changes independently of the agent's actions.

Example: A soccer-playing robot facing opponents who are trying to steal the ball.

Impact on Agents:

Static environments let agents "freeze time" and deliberate without panic. Dynamic ones require quick reflexes and constant re-perception to keep up.

Discrete vs. Continuous

Discrete: There are a finite number of possible states and actions.

Example: A checkers game—specific moves, clear positions.

Continuous: Infinite possibilities exist for states and actions.

Example: Controlling a drone's flight path—speed, angle, wind resistance, battery levels all vary on continuous scales.

Impact on Agents:

Discrete environments lend themselves to search trees and combinatorial planning. Continuous ones often need complex control algorithms, differential equations, and a lot more math than most of us want to deal with before coffee.

Other "Fun" Environment Challenges

Sometimes environments are also:

Multiagent: Multiple agents (collaborating or competing) share the same world.

Adversarial: Some agents actively work against you (hello, competitive gaming and cybersecurity).

Unknown: The rules of the environment themselves are unclear and must be learned on the fly.

You can imagine the complexity jumps when these factors are involved. It's the difference between "solve this maze" and "solve this maze while other players throw banana peels and the walls randomly rearrange themselves every 30 seconds."

Matching Agents to Environments

One of the most important jobs for an AI engineer (that's me, still covered in cat fur) is matching the agent's design to the environment.

A simple reflex agent might be fine for a static, fully observable, deterministic environment.

A planning, model-based, learning agent is needed for dynamic, partially observable, stochastic environments.

In short:

Different battles need different swords.

Trying to use a simple agent in a complex environment is like sending a garden snail to win a Formula 1 race. You'll get points for creativity, but not results.

Closing Loop: Environments Shape Intelligence

So here's the big idea: the environment isn't just where an agent acts—it's what shapes its intelligence.
The smarter the environment, the smarter the agent must be.

And hey, if your agent ever seems confused or slow, don't blame it immediately. Maybe it's just trying to survive in an environment where, for all it knows, gravity might randomly reverse every third Tuesday.

Welcome to building AI agents, folks. It's messy, it's hilarious, it's occasionally chaotic— and it's the best job in the world.

Now, if you'll excuse me, I need to rescue my cat, who just created a new "dynamic, stochastic, partially observable" environment by knocking over my coffee mug. Again.

Chapter 2: Core Components of an AI Agent

Imagine building a robot with no sensors and asking it to navigate rush-hour traffic. That's like trying to play chess blindfolded on a trampoline. In this chapter, we crack open the metaphorical robot skull and peek inside. What gives an AI agent its senses, its muscles, its brain? How do agents see the world, take action, and—most importantly—decide when not to walk into a wall?

This chapter delves into the fundamental building blocks of AI agents. It covers perception through sensors, the role of actuators in executing actions, and the varying architectures that dictate how agents process information and respond. We also explore how knowledge representation enables reasoning, and we analyze decision-making systems that allow agents to formulate plans and achieve goals in dynamic environments.

2.1 Perception and Sensors

Have you ever walked into a room, sniffed the air, and immediately decided "Yeah, something burned here"? Congratulations—you've just demonstrated perception in action. Your nose acted as a sensor, your brain processed the input, and you made a judgment about your environment.

AI agents aren't much different. Well, they don't have noses (yet—I'm still working on SmellNet 3000), but they do have sensors that allow them to gather information and make sense of the world around them. Without perception, an AI agent would be about as useful as a blindfolded dog trying to herd invisible sheep.

Today, we're cracking open the wonderful world of Perception and Sensors, where agents learn to stop guessing and start seeing. Or hearing. Or feeling. Or... you get the point.

What Is Perception in AI Agents?

At its core, perception is the process of taking raw sensory data and transforming it into something meaningful an agent can use to make decisions.

Imagine standing at a street corner:

Your eyes pick up shapes and colors (raw data).

Your brain recognizes a red octagon as a STOP sign (interpreted meaning).

You decide not to walk into oncoming traffic (action based on perception).

For AI agents, perception bridges the gap between the raw chaotic universe and structured, actionable understanding. Without it, agents would be blindly executing actions, often hilariously (and dangerously) wrong ones.

What Are Sensors?

Sensors are the tools agents use to perceive the environment. Think of them as the agent's eyes, ears, nose, skin, and tongue.

(Though, to be honest, I haven't yet met an AI agent that needed to taste anything. But you never know—future restaurant bots, beware.)

Depending on the environment and tasks, an agent might have sensors like:

Cameras (for vision)

Microphones (for sound)

LIDAR (for depth and distance)

GPS (for location)

Accelerometers (for motion)

Temperature sensors (for heat detection)

Infrared sensors (for night vision ninja skills)

Sensors gather low-level data—like pixels, sound waves, magnetic fields, vibrations, or chemical signals—which the agent must then interpret through its perception system.

The Perception Pipeline: From Pixels to Plans

Here's a simple breakdown of how an agent perceives:

Sensing: Raw data acquisition (e.g., a camera captures an image).

Preprocessing: Clean and organize the data (e.g., adjusting brightness, removing noise).

Feature Extraction: Find important patterns (e.g., identifying edges, corners, colors).

Interpretation: Attach meaning (e.g., "that blob is a pedestrian").

Decision Integration: Feed perception results into decision-making modules (e.g., "STOP, don't run over the pedestrian!").

This is not a one-and-done deal. In dynamic environments, perception must happen continuously and quickly, like an agent's never-ending heartbeat.

Noisy Sensors and Imperfect Perception

Now, let's talk about the ugly truth:

Sensors lie. A lot.

Real-world sensors are:

Noisy

Inaccurate

Prone to malfunctions

Sometimes hilariously bad (looking at you, GPS that puts me in the middle of a river).

Thus, agents must be built to handle uncertainty. This is where techniques like sensor fusion, filtering (like Kalman filters), and probabilistic reasoning come into play.

Basically, if one sensor says "there's a wall" and another says "no wall here," the agent needs some brainpower to figure out who to trust—or at least how to hedge its bets.

Pro tip: Trust, but verify. Even in sensor world.

Active vs. Passive Perception

Agents can be passive or active in their perceptual habits:

Passive Perception: Simply collect whatever information the environment provides. Like a plant soaking up sunlight.

Active Perception: Actively move or manipulate sensors to gain better information. Like a security guard shining a flashlight into dark corners.

For example, a drone might tilt its camera to get a better view of an obstacle, or a robot might rotate on the spot to build a full 3D map of a room.

Active perception allows agents to resolve ambiguities and reduce uncertainty, at the cost of extra time, energy, and complexity.

(Kind of like when you open the fridge, don't immediately see the leftovers you want, and then move things around—active perception to rescue your dinner.)

Sensors Are Specific to Tasks

One of the biggest mistakes new AI developers make is thinking more sensors = better agent.

Nope.

An agent needs the right sensors for its specific environment and goals.

Example:

A Mars rover needs radiation detectors.

A warehouse robot needs barcode scanners.

A home assistant needs microphones and cameras.

My coffee-fetching robot needs a caffeine detector. (Still working on the prototype.)

Unnecessary sensors add cost, processing overhead, and complexity. Worse, irrelevant sensory data can confuse an agent. Always match your perception gear to your mission.

Real-World Applications of Perception

Let's take a world tour of cool examples:

Self-Driving Cars: Combine LIDAR, radar, ultrasonic sensors, and cameras to understand roads, cars, pedestrians, and traffic signs.

Healthcare Robots: Use imaging sensors to analyze patient conditions or guide surgical tools.

Smart Homes: Voice-activated assistants like Alexa use microphone arrays and natural language processing to figure out when you're shouting "Turn off the lights!" while fumbling with laundry.

Security Systems: Surveillance agents recognize faces, detect motion, and even "hear" gunshots or broken glass to trigger alarms.

In every case, strong perception capabilities make the difference between an agent being a helpful genius or a clueless nuisance.

In Summary (and a Quick Pep Talk)

Perception is what turns an agent from a blind guesser into an intelligent actor.
Sensors are its eyes and ears, but perception—true understanding—comes from the clever software that processes all that juicy data into meaning.

Without perception, an agent is just a well-dressed brick.

With it?

An agent can drive a car, fly a drone, beat humans at board games, detect early signs of disease—and maybe even find the nearest Starbucks faster than you can.

And remember: in life, just like in AI, good perception beats good guessing every single time.

Unless you're guessing lottery numbers—then, hey, good luck and call me when you win.

2.2 Actuators and Actions

Have you ever watched a robot vacuum cleaner dramatically fling itself off a staircase? That's an actuator at work, folks—just not a very smart one.

Welcome to the fun (and slightly chaotic) world of Actuators and Actions, where agents move, shake, push, pull, and occasionally crash into walls. If sensors are how an agent feels the world, then actuators are how it punches it (gently, if we're lucky). And let's be honest: all the perception in the world means nothing if an agent can't do something with it.

Today, we're cracking open the story of how agents go from thinking to doing—and why sometimes even the best ideas end up in a tangled heap of wires and broken dreams.

What Are Actuators?

In simple terms, actuators are the agent's muscles.

They're the mechanical (or virtual) parts that turn a decision into a real-world action.

Depending on the type of agent, actuators can be:

Motors (to move wheels or arms)

Servos (for fine movement control)

Hydraulic pistons (for heavy lifting)

Speakers (to produce sound)

Displays (to show information)

Digital outputs (for software agents, like sending a message or clicking a button)

Without actuators, an AI agent would basically be a couch philosopher—full of grand theories, but never lifting a finger to help.

Actions: The Final Step

An action is what happens when an agent uses its actuators to affect the environment.

Actions could include:

Moving forward

Grabbing an object

Speaking a sentence

Sending a text

Launching a drone

Every intelligent agent operates in a perception-action loop:

Sense the environment.

Decide what to do.

Use actuators to perform an action.

Observe the new state of the environment.

Repeat until victory (or glorious failure).

It's basically the life cycle of every toddler ever—but with more math.

The Types of Actions

Depending on the complexity of the agent, actions can be simple or sophisticated:

Primitive Actions: Basic, low-level moves. Like "move left one step" or "grip object."

Composite Actions: Sequences of primitive actions stitched together. Like "pick up the cup, carry it to the table, and set it down gently."

In real-world systems, even seemingly "simple" actions often require coordinating dozens (or hundreds) of tiny actuator commands.

Example:

For a robotic arm to pick up a coffee mug, it must:

Move joints precisely

Adjust grip strength

Balance weight

Avoid knocking over nearby objects

(And if it's my personal robot, also avoid knocking over me because that apparently happens now.)

Challenges with Actuators and Actions

Life is messy. Actuators are messier.

Here are some problems engineers like me face regularly:

Inaccuracy: Motors don't move exactly the right distance.

Latency: There's a delay between issuing a command and seeing a response.

Wear and Tear: Physical parts break down over time.

Environmental Influence: Temperature, humidity, and terrain can all mess with actuators.

Energy Consumption: Every movement costs precious battery life or fuel.

That's why most real-world agents must continuously recalibrate based on feedback, adjusting their actions dynamically rather than trusting that everything worked perfectly the first time.

(It's a bit like checking if your email really sent... but for robots.)

Mapping Actions to Goals

An agent's actions must align with its goals—otherwise, you get a lot of movement but very little achievement.

Example:

Goal: Clean the floor.

Bad action: Spin in circles and beep loudly.

Good action: Move in straight lines, cover every area, avoid obstacles.

Effective agents use planning systems to decide which sequence of actions will get them closer to their goals. This might involve:

Pathfinding algorithms (e.g., A*)

Trajectory optimization

Decision trees

Reinforcement learning

Because remember, it's not about doing something—it's about doing the right thing at the right time.

Real-World Examples

Let's look at some cool real-world actuator-action combos:

Self-Driving Cars:

Actuators control steering, braking, acceleration, turn signals, horn honking (preferably not all at once).

Drone Delivery Robots:

Actuators adjust propeller speeds for flying, cargo hooks for grabbing packages, and cameras for adjusting altitude.

Smart Home Assistants:

Actuators control speakers, displays, and connected devices (like turning your lights off when you forget for the hundredth time).

Industrial Robots:

Precision motors and arms assemble products at lightning speed—with fewer coffee breaks than their human coworkers.

Each of these systems converts intelligence into physical or digital action. Without actuators, all those smart algorithms would just sit there, staring into the void.

Software Agents and Virtual Actions

Now, what about agents that aren't made of metal and wires?

Software agents, like chatbots or trading bots, also have "actuators"—just digital ones:

Sending messages

Making API calls

Executing trades

Updating databases

In these cases, the "action" affects a virtual environment instead of a physical one.
(And trust me, a financial trading bot can wreak just as much havoc as a runaway robot arm if it's not properly controlled.)

Actuators + Perception = The Dream Team

Here's the beautiful synergy:

Sensors pull in data.

Perception makes sense of it.

Decision-making modules choose what to do.

Actuators make it real.

Each part is essential. Miss one, and you're back to either a brain in a jar or a headless chicken.

A beautifully designed agent balances these systems like a well-trained acrobat balancing on a tightrope—except the acrobat is also solving calculus problems midair.

Final Thoughts (and a Slightly Dramatic Exit)

In short, actuators are what let agents move mountains (sometimes literally).

They transform intelligence into impact.

They're the difference between "knowing" and "doing."

And let's be real: in life, as in AI, you can have the best ideas in the world—but if you don't act, you're just another genius shouting into the void.

So go forth. Sense the world. Make decisions. Act boldly.

And if you crash into a wall now and then? Hey, at least you're moving.

(Which is more than I can say for my coffee robot. Still waiting, Steve.)

2.3 Agent Architecture: Rule-Based to Learning-Based

Picture this: you're building your very first AI agent. You're excited, you're caffeinated, you're ready to change the world. You fire up your laptop, crack your knuckles... and then realize you have absolutely no idea how to structure your agent's brain.

Welcome to the magical, slightly confusing land of Agent Architecture—the blueprint that decides how your agent thinks, decides, and acts.

Today, we're going to embark on a journey from the old-school Rule-Based agents who followed orders like obedient little robots, to the modern Learning-Based agents who— let's be honest—sometimes feel a little too independent for their own good.

Hold on to your design documents—we're diving deep.

What Is Agent Architecture?

At its simplest, agent architecture is the underlying design philosophy that defines:

How an agent perceives information

How it processes that information

How it makes decisions

How it acts in the world

Think of it like the internal wiring of your brain (minus the existential dread and questionable late-night snack decisions).

Choosing the right architecture is crucial because it impacts:

The agent's ability to react quickly

The complexity of behaviors it can exhibit

How easily it can adapt or learn

How scalable and maintainable it is over time

Bad architecture = Bad agent. No matter how shiny your sensors and actuators are.

The Classic: Rule-Based Agents

Let's start at the beginning—Rule-Based Agents.

These are the "if this, then that" bots. Simple, predictable, and about as rebellious as a wet sponge.

How they work:

You, the all-knowing designer, hand-code a list of rules.

When the agent perceives a situation, it finds the matching rule and executes the corresponding action.

Example:

IF light level < threshold → THEN turn on light

IF obstacle detected ahead → THEN stop moving

This is a lot like how we train toddlers:

"If you see a puddle, don't jump into it." (Spoiler: they jump anyway.)

Pros of Rule-Based Systems:

Simple to implement

Easy to debug

Highly predictable behavior

Cons:

Brittle—if a situation isn't explicitly covered by a rule, the agent freezes or fails

Hard to scale—managing hundreds or thousands of rules quickly becomes a nightmare

Dumb—no learning or adapting

Rule-Based Agents are fine for small, predictable environments. But as soon as things get messy?

They fall apart faster than a dollar-store lawn chair in a windstorm.

The Upgrade: Model-Based Agents

Feeling fancy? Then you might move up to Model-Based Reflex Agents.

These agents keep an internal model of the world.

Instead of just reacting to immediate sensor inputs, they think about how the world works.

How they work:

Maintain a belief about the environment's current state

Update this belief based on perceptions

Make decisions based on their internal model and goals

This allows them to handle partially observable environments much better.

(Unlike my cat, who still thinks the fridge disappears when I close the door.)

Pros:

Smarter reactions

Can reason about unseen parts of the environment

Cons:

More complex architecture

Still relies heavily on human-provided models

The Big Brains: Goal-Based and Utility-Based Agents

Now we're getting into aspirational territory.

Instead of just reacting to stuff, these agents set goals and plan actions to achieve them.

Goal-Based Agents:

Know what they want

Search for a sequence of actions to reach their goals

Utility-Based Agents:

Not only achieve goals but also optimize outcomes

Assign scores (utilities) to outcomes and pick the best one

Example:

A delivery drone could have the goal "deliver package," but also use utility functions to optimize for "least energy used" or "least likely to get attacked by angry birds."

Pros:

Flexible

Can handle complex, dynamic environments

More autonomous

Cons:

Needs powerful planning algorithms

More computationally expensive

Still relatively "rigid" if not combined with learning

The Revolution: Learning-Based Agents

Finally, we arrive at the cool kids on the block: Learning-Based Agents.

These agents don't need you to spoon-feed them rules or handcraft models. They learn from data, experiences, feedback, and mistakes.

Types of learning methods:

Supervised learning (learn from labeled data)

Unsupervised learning (find patterns in data)

Reinforcement learning (learn through trial and error with rewards)

How they work:

Start ignorant (just like human babies and most interns)

Gather experience

Improve their models and behaviors over time

Example:

A self-driving car agent learns to avoid potholes not because you told it how to spot every single pothole—but because it experienced the pain (bump) of hitting one and got smarter about it.

Pros:

Adaptability

Scalability

Potential for discovering new strategies humans didn't think of

Cons:

Requires large amounts of data

Training can be expensive and time-consuming

Sometimes unpredictable or "black-box" behavior

But honestly? Watching a Learning-Based Agent go from clueless noob to semi-intelligent operator is one of the most beautiful nerd experiences ever.

It's like teaching a puppy to sit—except the puppy eventually invents quantum computing. (Maybe.)

Choosing the Right Architecture

So, how do you pick the right architecture for your agent?

Ask yourself:

How complex is the environment?

How dynamic or unpredictable is it?

Does the agent need to adapt or is it fine to hardcode rules?

How much computational power and data do you have?

Sometimes, the best answer is a hybrid—mixing rule-based logic for simple tasks with learning-based modules for complex decisions.

(A bit like humans: "always brush your teeth" is hardcoded; "how to survive a zombie apocalypse" is learned on the fly.)

Final Thoughts (and a Poor Life Choice)

So, in conclusion:

Architecture matters. A lot.

Rule-based, model-based, goal-based, learning-based—they're all tools in your toolbox. Pick wisely based on your task, your environment, and your agent's dreams of digital glory.

And remember:

Even the best architecture won't save you if you train your agent to fetch coffee—and it brings you decaf.

(Which, frankly, should be considered a critical system failure.)

2.4 The Role of Knowledge Representation

Imagine this: you build the world's smartest AI agent. It can perceive, it can plan, it can act. You ask it, "Hey buddy, where's the nearest coffee shop?" and it just stares blankly into the digital void.

Why?

Because you forgot to teach it how to represent knowledge.

Oops.

Welcome to the wonderful (and slightly mind-bending) world of Knowledge Representation—the secret sauce that allows agents to think, reason, remember, and not look completely clueless when life throws curveballs.

Strap in. We're going to dive deep into how smart agents know what they know—and why without it, they're about as useful as a screen door on a submarine.

What Is Knowledge Representation?

At its core, Knowledge Representation (KR) is about how an agent structures information internally so it can:

Understand it

Reason with it

Retrieve it when needed

Use it to make decisions

It's basically the agent's mental filing system—but hopefully a lot more organized than your junk drawer at home.

Without knowledge representation, an agent is like a tourist with no map, no language skills, and no clue why everyone's yelling at them in traffic.

Why Knowledge Matters for AI Agents

Knowledge isn't just about facts ("Paris is the capital of France"); it's about relationships, causes and effects, categories, rules, exceptions, and sometimes even uncertainties.

Agents need knowledge to:

Predict outcomes ("If I turn left, I'll avoid that obstacle")

Generalize from experience ("Dogs are generally friendly, but that one with the spiky collar is not")

Plan actions ("If I'm hungry, I should go to the fridge before I start cooking")

Handle ambiguous situations ("Did Bob mean literal fire when he said the party was lit?")

In short: intelligent behavior = good knowledge representation.

Otherwise, your AI agent will be that guy at trivia night who thinks Einstein invented the burrito.

Forms of Knowledge Representation

Let's break down a few popular ways agents represent knowledge:

1. Logical Representation

Think First-Order Logic (FOL)

Facts and relationships are encoded as logical statements.

Example: "All cats are mammals. Whiskers is a cat. Therefore, Whiskers is a mammal."

Pros:

Precise, powerful for reasoning.

Cons:

Can be rigid and hard to scale in complex, noisy environments.

2. Semantic Networks

Knowledge is stored as a graph of nodes and edges.

Nodes represent concepts; edges represent relationships.

Example: [Dog] —is a—> [Animal]

Pros:

Visual, intuitive.

Great for hierarchical knowledge.

Cons:

Not ideal for handling uncertainty.

3. Frames

Like object-oriented programming for knowledge.

Frames group related facts together into "templates."

Example: A "Restaurant" frame might include fields for location, cuisine, price range.

Pros:

Modular and easy to extend.

Cons:

Not great for complex dynamic reasoning.

4. Production Rules

"IF condition THEN action" rules.

Example: IF "It's raining" THEN "Carry an umbrella."

Pros:

Simple, good for reactive systems.

Cons:

Can become spaghetti mess if too many rules pile up.

5. Ontologies

Formal, structured frameworks for organizing knowledge domains.

Example: Medical ontologies categorize diseases, symptoms, treatments.

Pros:

Super powerful for big, structured systems (like healthcare or finance).

Cons:

Building and maintaining ontologies is... let's just say, not for the faint-hearted.

How Agents Use Knowledge Representation

Knowledge isn't just for show—it's a working asset.

Agents use KR for:

Inference: Drawing conclusions based on known facts.

Decision Making: Choosing between different actions.

Planning: Figuring out sequences of actions to reach a goal.

Learning: Updating the knowledge base with new information.

Example:

A cleaning robot needs to know:

Where rooms are located (spatial knowledge)

How to detect dirt (sensor knowledge)

Which areas are off-limits (rule knowledge)

Without structured knowledge, it's just going to spin in circles looking confused.

(Kind of like me trying to find the clean laundry I swear I folded yesterday.)

Challenges in Knowledge Representation

KR is powerful, but it's also tricky business. Some of the challenges include:

Incomplete knowledge: Agents often don't have full information.

Uncertain knowledge: Sensor readings are noisy; humans are vague ("It's kind of chilly"—okay, but what's the actual temperature?).

Changing environments: What an agent "knows" might become outdated (today's open road becomes tomorrow's construction zone).

Computational complexity: Reasoning with massive knowledge bases can slow agents down.

Good KR systems balance expressiveness (being able to represent lots of kinds of knowledge) with efficiency (being able to reason fast enough to act).

The Evolution Toward Learning-Based Knowledge

In modern AI, agents increasingly learn their knowledge representations from data rather than having everything manually coded.

Deep learning models like neural networks represent knowledge in a very different way— through distributed representations across millions of tiny weights.

The upside?

Scalability

Flexibility

Ability to handle noisy, complex environments

The downside?

Lack of transparency (it's often hard to tell what exactly the agent knows)

Hard to debug ("Why did the self-driving car think that stop sign was a hippo??")

Final Thoughts (and a Slight Existential Crisis)

In summary:

Without good knowledge representation, agents are helpless.

With it, they become adaptable, reasoning, semi-genius beings ready to tackle complex real-world challenges.

If building AI agents is like raising children, then teaching them how to represent knowledge is the part where you hand them a backpack, a notebook, and a vague warning not to eat glue.

And remember:

Even the smartest AI agent can't help you if it doesn't know the difference between "save the cat" and "save from the cat."

(Trust me. Been there. Got the claw marks.)

2.5 Decision-Making and Planning Systems

Ever stood in front of your fridge at midnight, torn between leftover pizza and a sad, lonely apple? Congratulations, you've experienced decision-making and planning—two things AI agents have to deal with all the time (minus the pizza, sadly).

In this chapter, we're going to explore how AI agents actually choose actions and plan for the future instead of just reacting like confused squirrels.

Because let's be honest: without good decision-making, even the smartest agent ends up looking like a Roomba stuck under a couch—ambitious, but tragically ineffective.

Buckle up, planner-in-training. It's time to turn our agents into proactive geniuses, not reactive disasters.

What is Decision-Making in AI Agents?

At its core, decision-making is about an agent figuring out what to do next based on:

What it knows (perceptions, internal knowledge)

What it wants (goals, utilities)

What's possible (available actions)

It's like constantly playing a personal game of chess with the universe—except sometimes the pieces move by themselves and the rules change mid-game.

Good decision-making ensures the agent acts rationally and purposefully, not just flailing around like it's auditioning for a bad reality show.

How Agents Make Decisions

There are several ways an agent can make decisions, depending on how smart (and how lazy) you want it to be:

1. Simple Rule-Based Decisions

"If I see danger, run."

"If battery low, recharge."

No deep thinking—just automatic responses based on pre-set rules.

Good for:

Simple, fast reactions

Highly predictable behavior

Bad for:

Complex, dynamic environments where rigid rules won't cut it

(Kind of like those people who only ever order chicken nuggets no matter which restaurant they're at.)

2. Decision Trees

A tree structure where each branch represents a decision or test.

Follow the branches based on current conditions to reach an action.

Example:

Battery low? Yes → Near charger? No → Search for charger.

Good for:

More nuanced decision-making than basic rules

Visualizing possible actions and outcomes

Bad for:

Huge, complex scenarios (tree gets monstrous fast)

Fun fact: real trees don't make decisions, but decision trees definitely branch out faster than you can say "combinatorial explosion."

3. Utility-Based Decision-Making

The agent scores possible outcomes based on a utility function (how "good" or "bad" they are).

Chooses the action that maximizes expected utility.

Example:

If "get coffee" has a utility of +10 and "stay sleepy" has a utility of -5, the agent will bravely venture out for caffeine.

Good for:

Handling trade-offs and multiple goals

Flexible behavior in uncertain environments

Bad for:

Requires careful design of utility functions (otherwise, agents might prioritize weird stuff... like building 500 chairs instead of just finding a seat)

4. Learning-Based Decision-Making

Instead of manually defining utilities or rules, agents learn optimal decisions from data.

Reinforcement learning is a common approach (reward good actions, punish bad ones).

Example:

A robot that learns by trial and error how best to stack boxes without toppling them (or itself).

Good for:

Complex, unpredictable environments

Adapting to new situations without manual reprogramming

Bad for:

Requires lots of experience

Sometimes makes hilariously (or horrifyingly) bad decisions at first

(Kind of like toddlers learning to walk: a lot of falling, crying, and occasionally impressive feats of agility.)

What is Planning in AI Agents?

Planning is about looking ahead—not just making the next move, but figuring out a whole sequence of moves to reach a goal.

Agents that plan aren't just reacting to the world; they're strategizing. They're asking:

"Where am I now?"

"Where do I want to be?"

"What steps do I need to get there?"

Planning turns random movement into purposeful action, which turns AI agents into actual problem solvers instead of glorified bumper cars.

Types of Planning Systems

1. Classical Planning

Assumes a perfect, predictable world.

You know the full state of the world and the effects of all actions.

Example: Chess programs use classical planning.

Methods:

State-space search: Searching through all possible states.

Plan-space search: Searching through sequences of actions.

Good for:

Highly controlled environments

Bad for:

Real-world messiness (where things break, change, or lie to you)

2. Hierarchical Planning

Breaks down big goals into smaller sub-goals.

Focus on "what needs to happen first" before tackling high-level objectives.

Example:

"Make dinner" → "Buy groceries" → "Cook ingredients" → "Eat while binge-watching."

Good for:

Managing complexity

Easier scaling for bigger tasks

Bad for:

Still assumes a relatively stable environment

3. Contingency Planning

Planning for what could go wrong.

Include "Plan B" (and sometimes C, D, and E) just in case things don't go perfectly.

Example:

"If my path to the charging station is blocked, find an alternative route."

Good for:

Uncertain or risky environments

Bad for:

Computationally expensive (so many contingencies!)

Basically, it's like bringing an umbrella because you might get rained on—and packing a snow shovel because you might get a surprise blizzard.

4. Real-Time Planning

Planning on the fly as the agent moves through the environment.

Focused on speed and adaptability rather than perfect plans.

Good for:

Fast-paced environments (robot soccer, real-time strategy games)

Bad for:

No guarantee of the best possible solution, just "good enough" to survive

Sometimes you gotta move fast and figure it out later—just like cramming for a final exam with two hours of sleep and three Red Bulls.

Decision-Making vs. Planning: The Dynamic Duo

In practice, decision-making and planning are tightly linked:

Planning creates a map ("here's the best path to the goal")

Decision-making navigates that map ("at this intersection, turn left")

A good agent can switch between long-term planning and short-term decision-making fluidly, like a GPS that recalculates after you make a wrong turn (or three).

Final Thoughts (and Questionable Life Advice)

In conclusion:

Good decision-making lets your agent pick smart actions.

Good planning lets your agent chain those actions into winning strategies.

Master both, and you get agents that don't just survive—they thrive.

And if you ever find yourself stuck between leftover pizza and a sad apple again?

Remember: Planning says, "Eat the apple now, enjoy longer life."

Decision-making says, "Eat pizza now, enjoy happiness today."

Choose wisely.

(Some of us are still choosing pizza. No regrets.)

Chapter 3: Classifying AI Agents

Let's talk personalities. Some agents react like startled cats, others plan like chess grandmasters, and a few are constantly learning like toddlers hopped up on sugar and curiosity. This chapter is your crash course in AI agent taxonomy—a digital safari where we spot reflex agents, model-based thinkers, and utility-obsessed decision-makers in their natural habitats. Bonus points if you can tell them apart without getting bitten.

Formally, this chapter categorizes AI agents based on their internal complexity and capabilities. We discuss simple reflex agents, model-based reflex agents, goal-based and utility-based agents, as well as adaptive learning agents. Finally, we introduce hybrid architectures that combine elements of different models for improved flexibility and performance in complex environments.

3.1 Simple Reflex Agents

Alright, let's set the stage: imagine building a robot. You want it to look impressive, act smart... and it immediately bumps into the wall because it doesn't think—it just reacts. Congratulations, you've built your very first Simple Reflex Agent.

Simple reflex agents are the "see something, do something" of the AI world. No deep thinking. No existential crises. Just pure action, baby.
They are the AI equivalent of that one friend who always claps at the end of movies no matter what.

In this chapter, we'll explore these wonderfully straightforward agents—where they shine, where they flop, and why sometimes "thinking too much" is not only unnecessary but downright disastrous.

What is a Simple Reflex Agent?

A Simple Reflex Agent is an AI system that acts solely based on its current perception, without any regard for the past or consideration of the future.
It uses a set of condition-action rules to determine its behavior.

In human terms:

- "If I see rain → open umbrella."

- "If I see a red light → stop."

- "If I smell cookies → steal cookies."

No memory. No learning. No questions asked.

Simple reflex agents operate under the philosophy of "if it ain't broke, don't fix it"—only, if it is broke, they probably won't notice.

How Simple Reflex Agents Work

At their core, these agents follow a straightforward loop:

Perceive the environment.

Match the perception to a rule.

Act according to the matched rule.

That's it.

No storing past information. No predicting future consequences. Just straight-up action based on the now.

Here's a tiny blueprint of how their brain (if you can call it that) functions:

function Simple-Reflex-Agent(percept) returns an action:
   rule <- Rule-Matching-Function(percept, rule-base)
   return action associated with rule

It's the AI version of muscle memory: stimulus in, response out.

A Real-World Example: The Roomba

Let's talk about everyone's favorite little disk-shaped buddy: the Roomba.

Early Roombas are a great example of simple reflex agents:

Bump into wall → Turn randomly.

See dirt → Vacuum.

Battery low → Search for dock.

They don't map the room. They don't remember where they've been.

They just react to the immediate stimuli—and yet somehow, they manage to clean the floor (eventually).

Sure, it's not elegant.

Sure, sometimes it attacks your dog.

But hey, it works.

Strengths of Simple Reflex Agents

Despite sounding dumber than a box of hammers, simple reflex agents have their place:

Speed: Lightning-fast decisions because there's no processing overhead.

Simplicity: Easy to design, easy to troubleshoot.

Reliability: In stable environments, they do exactly what you expect.

Cost-Effective: Great for cheap devices that don't need to overthink.

Imagine trying to make a coffee machine that "plans" its brewing strategy. No.

Push button → Brew coffee → Everyone's happy.

Simple wins sometimes.

Weaknesses of Simple Reflex Agents

But oh boy, do these agents have limitations:

Zero Memory: They can't learn from past mistakes.

Zero Prediction: They don't think ahead at all.

Fragility: If the environment changes unexpectedly, they fail spectacularly.

Limited Flexibility: New situations outside their rule set confuse them utterly.

Imagine if your self-driving car was a simple reflex agent:

"See red → stop. See green → go."

Now imagine a construction site, a detour sign, a guy dressed as a traffic cone.

Yeah. Total meltdown.

Simple reflex agents are great until things get even slightly complicated.

When to Use Simple Reflex Agents

Simple reflex agents are surprisingly effective in fully observable, highly predictable environments.

Perfect use cases include:

Basic automation (lights turn on when motion detected)

Entry-level robotics (line-following bots)

Appliances (microwaves, coffee makers, smart fans)

If the world is simple and the task is repetitive, you don't need a genius—just a good reflex.

On the other hand, if your environment is messy, dynamic, or filled with surprises (like, say, anywhere humans exist)...

You're going to need something smarter.

Building a Simple Reflex Agent: Quick Framework

If you ever want to build one (for fun, for science, for taking over your living room Roomba army), the recipe looks like this:

Define Percepts: What sensory input can the agent receive?

Set Up Condition-Action Rules: Map percepts to actions.

Implement Rule Matching: Match current percept to a rule.

Execute Action: Carry out the matched action immediately.

That's it. No databases. No machine learning.

Just sweet, sweet knee-jerk reactions.

Example for a basic light control agent:

Percept	Action
Dark	Turn light ON
Bright	Turn light OFF

Simple Reflex Agents in Pop Culture

Honestly, tons of movie robots started life as simple reflex agents before their writers decided to make them sentient.

Early R2-D2? Basically a noisy reflex agent.

- The house AI in Smart House (before it went rogue)? Reflex agent.
- That old vending machine that ate your dollar? Definitely a reflex agent. Possibly evil.

Final Thoughts (and a Small Existential Crisis)

Simple reflex agents teach us an important lesson:

You don't always need to be smart to be effective.

Sometimes just responding quickly and predictably is better than overthinking every choice. (Take note, indecisive late-night snackers.)

But if you want to survive in a wild, messy world full of unexpected twists, you'd better pack more than just reflexes.

You'll need memory, prediction, learning... basically, a brain bigger than a walnut.

Until then, there's a special charm in agents who keep it simple.

Just like me reflexively saying "yes" to dessert without a second thought.

(Zero regrets. Maximum satisfaction.)

3.2 Model-Based Reflex Agents

Alright, so last time, we met the Simple Reflex Agent, which was essentially the "shoot first, ask questions never" type.

Now, let's bump things up a notch: Model-Based Reflex Agents.

These agents are like the more responsible sibling who doesn't just react based on what's happening right now. Nope, these agents remember a few things from the past and use that info to make smarter decisions in the present. They've got their head in the game and don't just forget that they're stuck in a maze—again.

So, imagine you're driving a car. You don't just react to what's happening in the moment; you have a mental map of the road. Maybe you remember the stop signs you passed a few minutes ago, or how fast you were going. This "map" helps you avoid doing something dumb, like driving into a lake. Model-Based Reflex Agents are essentially cars with memory, trying not to drive into metaphorical lakes.

What is a Model-Based Reflex Agent?

A Model-Based Reflex Agent is like the "thinker" in the world of reflex agents. They don't just blindly respond to their environment—they use internal models of the world (or at least their environment) to inform their actions.

In other words, instead of just reacting based on what's happening in the current moment (like a simple reflex agent), these agents remember some key details about the environment. They can then make better decisions based on the state of the world and how it has changed over time.

Here's an example:

You're playing a game where you need to collect treasure in a dungeon.

A simple reflex agent would just wander around, reacting to its immediate surroundings (find treasure, pick it up, run away from monsters).

A model-based reflex agent, however, would remember the layout of the dungeon as it explores, track where it's been, and use that information to avoid running in circles or getting trapped by monsters. It has a mental map that guides its decision-making.

So, while simple reflex agents are all about the here and now, model-based reflex agents keep a mental record of the world and use it to make more informed, effective decisions.

How Do Model-Based Reflex Agents Work?

Here's the magic behind the scenes:

Perception: The agent senses the environment.

Model Update: It updates its internal model of the world based on the current perception.

Rule Matching: The agent checks its rule base, using the model and current perception to find the most appropriate action.

Action: The agent takes action based on the matched rule.

It's like when you're trying to remember the name of a movie you watched last year. You might not recall the exact details, but you can remember who starred in it or what the plot was about. Using that mental model, you narrow down the possibilities. That's the internal model helping out.

Model-based reflex agents use state representation to keep track of the world and update it as they interact with it. This internal model lets the agent figure out the best move, even when it doesn't have all the information about the current environment. It's like playing chess with an incomplete board but having a rough idea of where the pieces are.

Key Features of Model-Based Reflex Agents

Memory: Unlike simple reflex agents, model-based reflex agents remember things. They keep track of the state of the world (a model) and use it to make better decisions.

Internal Model: The agent builds and updates a model of its environment to understand how it's changing over time. This allows it to adapt to new situations and avoid repeating mistakes.

Condition-Action Rules: The agent still uses condition-action rules, but these rules are based on both the current environment and the internal model of past experiences.

State Representation: The agent tracks the environment's state, which might include objects, locations, or other important details. If the agent moves through a room, it updates its knowledge of where it is, and what it has encountered.

The Internals: How It Works in Code (Simplified)

Here's how a simple model-based reflex agent might work:

function Model-Based-Reflex-Agent(percept) returns an action:
    state = Update-Model(state, percept)   // Update the internal model
    rule = Rule-Matching(state)   // Match the current state to an action
    return action   // Execute the chosen action

The key part here is the Update-Model function, which keeps the agent's internal state updated based on the latest perceptions. This makes the agent aware of what happened before, so it doesn't just blindly react.

Think of it like tracking your stock portfolio—just because you saw a dip in prices doesn't mean you panic-sell. Instead, you look at the model of your portfolio's performance and then decide whether it's worth holding, buying more, or cutting your losses. The agent's model lets it make decisions based on past experiences and the present state of the environment.

Strengths of Model-Based Reflex Agents

These agents have a few key advantages over their simpler counterparts:

Memory of Past States: They don't just react to the world as it is right now. They remember past states and learn from them.

More Effective in Complex Environments: In environments where the world changes, agents need to keep track of what's going on to avoid repeating mistakes.

Flexibility: They can handle more complex scenarios, adapting their actions to fit the state of the environment.

For example, think of a robot vacuum with a map of your house. Unlike a simple reflex vacuum that might go in random directions, the model-based vacuum knows where it's already cleaned and where to go next. It's a little smarter and gets the job done more efficiently.

Weaknesses of Model-Based Reflex Agents

Of course, nothing's perfect. Here's what these agents might struggle with:

Still Limited in Complex, Dynamic Environments: While better than simple reflex agents, they can still be overwhelmed if the environment is too unpredictable or constantly changing.

Cost of Memory: Keeping track of all the states and updating the model requires more computational resources than simple reflex agents. This can slow down the agent's decision-making if not optimized properly.

Incomplete or Incorrect Models: If the agent's model of the world is wrong or incomplete, it can lead to poor decision-making, just like when you remember the last pizza you ordered but forget you switched toppings last time.

It's like driving with a GPS that hasn't been updated in years. You might get to your destination, but be prepared for a few detours and wrong turns.

Practical Applications of Model-Based Reflex Agents

Model-based reflex agents work best in situations where:

The world is predictable but requires some tracking of changes over time.

There's a need to adapt actions based on past experiences or states.

Here are a few areas where they shine:

Autonomous robots (like warehouse robots that need to remember where they've already been)

Automated systems (like thermostat controls that adjust temperature based on previous behavior)

Game AI (like NPCs that track the player's location and remember actions they've taken)

They're smarter than simple reflex agents but still don't need to completely think like human beings. The agent is really just updating its "mental map" and reacting accordingly.

Final Thoughts (and a Shameless Comparison to Your Own Life)

In summary:

Model-Based Reflex Agents are like people who learn from their mistakes… kind of. They don't have an advanced brain or long-term memory, but they've got enough going on in their internal model to avoid slamming into walls (most of the time).

If you've ever adjusted your approach to a problem based on past experience—whether it's deciding to take the stairs instead of the elevator or learning to leave your house 10 minutes earlier to avoid traffic—you've used a model-based reflex strategy.

So, if simple reflex agents are the impulsive eaters of the AI world, model-based reflex agents are like those who at least remember to bring their lunch to work. They may not be able to plan a full meal for the week, but they'll definitely remember to avoid the hot dog stand after that last bad experience.

3.3 Goal-Based and Utility-Based Agents

Alright, imagine this scenario: You're setting out to complete a task. Not just any task, but a well-defined, specific goal that you'll complete no matter what. Maybe it's to bake a perfect cake, or maybe it's to finally conquer that half-finished video game that's been sitting on your shelf for too long.

Now, imagine you're an AI. Instead of just reacting to the environment like a reflex agent, you're actively chasing a goal—a specific outcome. And just to make things more exciting, you could also be deciding on the best possible way to achieve that goal based on your personal preferences or "utility."

This is where Goal-Based Agents and Utility-Based Agents come into play. Goal-based agents are like that determined friend who says, "I don't care what's in my way—I'm going to reach that goal!" On the other hand, utility-based agents are a bit more practical. They still have goals, but they make sure to find the most optimal and rewarding way to achieve them.

What Are Goal-Based Agents?

Goal-Based Agents are like the ultimate overachievers. They are designed with a clear, specific goal in mind, and they will use all the information available to them to achieve that goal. Think of a GPS navigation system: the goal is to get you from point A to point B, and everything it does is aimed at achieving that. It might take the fastest route, avoid traffic, or reroute if there's a roadblock ahead.

A goal in the context of an AI agent is a desired state that the agent is trying to reach. The agent will select actions based on whether or not they help it move closer to achieving that goal. These agents are much more dynamic than reflex agents because they must decide not only how to act in the present moment but also consider how their actions will influence the future. They have mental models of their environment and plans to reach their goals.

In simpler terms: a goal-based agent is like that one friend who can't just hang out without a plan. They're always talking about "getting to the next level" and are never content with just showing up.

What Are Utility-Based Agents?

While goal-based agents are pretty determined, utility-based agents bring a little practicality into the equation. If goal-based agents are the "just get it done" type, utility-based agents are like the people who do cost-benefit analysis before choosing a restaurant for lunch.

Utility in AI refers to the measure of how satisfying a particular state or outcome is to the agent. Instead of focusing solely on a single goal, utility-based agents choose actions that maximize their overall satisfaction. Think of it as choosing to get the most value out of every decision. This is similar to when you buy something on sale—you're still achieving a goal (getting the item), but you're maximizing the utility (getting a better deal).

A utility-based agent has a variety of possible states it can achieve, and instead of picking the first one it sees, it evaluates the utility of each possible action and picks the one that maximizes its happiness (or, in our case, its objective). For example, if an agent has several ways to get to a goal, it will choose the one that provides the highest reward—this could be the least effort, lowest cost, or greatest payoff.

In other words, utility-based agents are like the "what's in it for me" thinkers of the AI world. They want to achieve their goals, but they're going to pick the most efficient, rewarding route.

How Do Goal-Based and Utility-Based Agents Work?

Both types of agents rely on decision-making processes, but they approach it in different ways.

Goal-Based Agent Workflow:

The agent sets a specific goal or desired outcome.

It evaluates the current state of the environment and determines what needs to change.

It picks actions that will move it closer to the goal.

Once the goal is reached, the agent stops and celebrates (in its own AI way).

A simple goal-based agent might be a robot vacuum cleaner that has the goal of covering the entire floor. It doesn't care about the efficiency—it just needs to make sure that it reaches every corner.

Utility-Based Agent Workflow:

The agent identifies a set of possible goals or outcomes.

It evaluates the utility or satisfaction of each possible outcome.

It picks the action that maximizes its utility (the most satisfying result).

The agent adjusts its decision-making based on feedback from the environment and maximizes satisfaction over time.

Imagine a shopping assistant AI that helps you buy a laptop. Instead of just picking the cheapest laptop (which could be a goal), it factors in things like value for money, features, and user reviews—maximizing its utility by helping you make the best purchase possible.

Strengths of Goal-Based Agents

Focused Objective: These agents have a clear goal they're trying to achieve, making them easy to define and track.

Clear Decision Making: Since the agent knows what it's trying to achieve, it can always focus on actions that move it closer to the goal.

Great for Well-Defined Tasks: If the task is clear-cut (e.g., play chess, follow a path), goal-based agents are perfect.

If your goal is simply to win a game of chess, a goal-based agent will use the best strategy to win. It's like you're playing against a friend who's really bad at the game but determined to beat you by any means necessary.

Strengths of Utility-Based Agents

Flexibility: These agents are designed to handle more complex situations because they can consider multiple goals and choose actions based on maximizing utility.

More Adaptive: Because utility-based agents don't just focus on a single goal, they can adapt to changing environments and new circumstances.

Better in Uncertainty: When there are multiple ways to reach a goal, utility-based agents can evaluate the trade-offs and pick the most efficient route, making them more effective in uncertain or dynamic environments.

A smart thermostat that adjusts your home's temperature might use utility-based decision-making. Instead of just sticking to one set goal (like a fixed temperature), it evaluates the current state (time of day, weather, occupancy) and optimizes comfort and energy savings.

Weaknesses of Goal-Based and Utility-Based Agents

While both agent types are incredibly useful, they have their drawbacks.

Goal-Based Agents:

Single Focus: They are only concerned with achieving one goal at a time, which can lead to inefficiency if there are multiple conflicting objectives.

Can Get Stuck: If something unexpected happens (like a roadblock), goal-based agents may fail because they don't have any strategy for handling the unexpected.

Utility-Based Agents:

Computation Overhead: Evaluating all possible outcomes to choose the one with the highest utility can be computationally expensive.

Trade-Off Complexity: Deciding between conflicting goals (like saving money vs. getting a premium product) can sometimes lead to difficult or suboptimal decisions.

When to Use Goal-Based vs Utility-Based Agents?

Use Goal-Based Agents when:

The task is simple, with a well-defined, clear objective.

You need a straightforward path to achieving a single goal.

Use Utility-Based Agents when:

The task involves multiple factors or competing goals.

You need to balance various objectives (e.g., cost vs. quality).

The environment is uncertain or constantly changing.

Conclusion: Where Do You Fit In?

Goal-based and utility-based agents are designed to handle a wide range of tasks—whether it's achieving a simple goal or optimizing actions for maximum benefit. In the world of AI, it's all about finding the right balance between determination (goal-based) and practicality (utility-based). So, whether you're chasing that perfect cup of coffee or deciding between the cheapest and most efficient route to get there, these agents are the secret sauce to making decisions that actually make sense.

For now, though, I'll let you go chase your own goals. Maybe pick the best route to your favorite snack? Just remember, the quickest path to happiness sometimes includes a little utility-based optimization... or just some chocolate.

3.4 Learning Agents

Alright, buckle up because we're about to talk about Learning Agents—and not the kind of learning where you just memorize some facts for a test and then promptly forget them after the bell rings. These agents are more like the students of life, constantly improving and adapting based on their experiences. Imagine an AI that is actively learning from its environment, tweaking its behavior, and getting better at whatever it's doing. Basically, AI that gets smarter over time, and we're not talking about just reading a manual and following rules.

These agents don't come pre-loaded with a set of answers—they have the ability to learn from experience, just like how you get better at cooking the more you burn those pancakes. The more data they collect, the better they become at predicting outcomes, making decisions, and avoiding mistakes. In fact, they might even start out as pretty terrible at what they do. But, over time, as they get feedback (whether it's rewards or penalties), they'll adapt and improve their strategies. It's like the AI version of the tortoise in The Tortoise and the Hare—slow and steady wins the race.

What is a Learning Agent?

A Learning Agent is, quite simply, an agent that improves its behavior over time based on feedback from its environment. Unlike goal-based agents, who just focus on achieving a specific goal, or reflex agents that blindly react, learning agents use a feedback loop to refine and optimize their actions over time.

Here's the deal:

A learning agent perceives its environment and takes actions based on what it learns.

It evaluates the outcome of those actions (through rewards or penalties).

It updates its model or strategy to improve future decisions, moving closer to optimal performance.

This is the essence of machine learning—but more on that in a bit. Think of it like learning to ride a bike. The first few tries are clumsy, you fall off, but eventually, after a couple of hundred crashes (and hopefully a helmet), you learn how to balance. A learning agent does the same thing—it gets feedback, adapts, and eventually, nails it.

The Key Components of a Learning Agent

To fully appreciate what makes learning agents tick, we need to break down their core components. Grab your imaginary clipboard—let's take notes:

Learning Element: This is the part of the agent that learns from its environment. It adapts its strategy based on feedback, and over time, it optimizes its actions. Imagine it as the agent's "brain"—the smarter it gets, the better its decisions will be.

Performance Element: This is the action-taker. It's the part of the agent that carries out the actual actions in the world, whether it's moving a robot's arm or making a decision in a video game. The performance element is directly impacted by what the learning element learns over time.

Critic: The critic gives feedback to the learning agent. It assesses how well the agent's actions align with the desired outcomes. If the agent does well, the critic provides positive feedback (a reward). If the agent does poorly, the critic gives negative feedback (a penalty). Think of it like the teacher who grades your homework—except this teacher is an AI that is constantly reminding you to do better next time.

Problem Generator: The problem generator introduces challenges or new problems to the agent to solve. The agent needs to deal with these new scenarios in order to improve its performance. This keeps the learning process fresh and encourages the agent to not just rest on its laurels but continuously strive for improvement.

This cycle of perceiving, acting, evaluating, and learning is what keeps a learning agent evolving and improving its strategies.

How Do Learning Agents Work?

A learning agent works by interacting with its environment, just like any other agent. But where it shines is its ability to improve over time. The process is similar to how we humans learn from experience.

Here's a basic breakdown:

Interaction: The agent perceives the current state of the environment and takes action based on its current knowledge. This could be anything from a robot moving through a room to a financial AI making trading decisions.

Feedback: After taking an action, the agent receives feedback from the environment (either positive or negative). This feedback is crucial because it helps the agent figure out whether it's getting closer to its goal or straying off course.

Learning: The learning element uses this feedback to update the agent's internal model of the world. This might involve changing how the agent perceives the environment, adjusting its decision-making process, or refining its approach to tasks.

Improvement: As the agent continues to interact with its environment, it gradually gets better at making decisions. The more feedback it gets, the more it improves. This process is known as reinforcement learning, where the agent learns from rewards and punishments.

It's like teaching a dog tricks: you start with simple commands, reward the dog when it does something right, and over time, it learns what to do to get the treat. Similarly, a learning agent starts with basic actions, receives feedback, and over time, its behavior becomes more optimized.

Types of Learning in Agents

There are several ways that learning can occur in agents, and these can be broadly categorized into a few types:

Supervised Learning: This is where the agent is given labeled data (with input-output pairs) and learns from that data. It's like having a mentor show you exactly how things should be done. For example, teaching an AI to recognize images of cats by showing it thousands of pictures labeled "cat" and "not cat."

Unsupervised Learning: In this scenario, the agent is given data but no explicit labels. It has to find patterns and structure in the data on its own. This is like being thrown into a new environment without a guide and learning to navigate it through trial and error. For example, clustering similar data points together without knowing exactly what the data represents.

Reinforcement Learning: Here's where things get exciting. The agent learns by interacting with its environment and receiving rewards or punishments. It doesn't have the luxury of labeled data; it's essentially learning by doing. For instance, a robot learning to walk will only know it's succeeding when it gets a reward (e.g., standing up or walking without falling over) or failing when it gets a penalty (e.g., falling over).

Deep Learning: This is a more advanced type of learning that uses neural networks to model complex patterns in data. It's like training an agent with a brain that can handle vast amounts of data and figure out incredibly complicated tasks. Deep learning has powered some of the most impressive AI systems we have today, like self-driving cars or AI that can play video games at a superhuman level.

Strengths of Learning Agents

Adaptability: Learning agents are able to adapt to new situations and environments because they learn over time. This makes them particularly useful for tasks that require flexibility.

Efficiency Over Time: The more the agent learns, the more efficient it becomes at solving problems. The learning process itself enables continuous improvement.

Autonomy: Learning agents don't need a lot of hand-holding. Once they've learned how to achieve their goals, they can work independently without human intervention.

Weaknesses of Learning Agents

Slow Start: At the beginning, learning agents might not perform well since they're essentially "starting from scratch." They need time to accumulate data and experience to become effective.

Resource-Intensive: The learning process requires computational power, especially when dealing with large amounts of data or complex environments. This can be costly in terms of time and resources.

Uncertainty: Sometimes, the feedback loop doesn't provide enough information for the agent to make clear decisions. If the environment is too unpredictable or if the reward signal is too weak, the agent might struggle to improve.

Practical Applications of Learning Agents

Learning agents are used in a variety of real-world applications, especially when adaptability and optimization are key:

Autonomous vehicles (learning how to navigate traffic)

Robotic systems (learning how to interact with their environment)

Game-playing AI (learning how to beat human players by improving through gameplay)

Recommendation systems (learning what movies, books, or products users are likely to enjoy)

These agents get better the more they interact with the world, just like a novice gamer who starts out bad but eventually learns to dominate the game.

Final Thoughts: The AI That Never Stops Learning

Learning agents are like that friend who's always evolving, always improving, and constantly growing from their experiences. They're not static—they learn, adapt, and get better the more they interact with their environment. In the world of AI, learning agents are the ultimate overachievers—never content to settle, always looking for new ways to optimize and improve.

So, next time you interact with a system that gets smarter over time, just remember: It might be learning, and one day, it might even be teaching you a thing or two. If you ever feel like an AI could do better, well... don't worry, it will! It's just in its nature.

3.5 Hybrid Architectures and Their Use Cases

Alright, let's talk Hybrid Architectures—you know, the kind of combination of multiple approaches that sounds like a sci-fi concept, but actually works pretty darn well in the real world. Hybrid architectures combine different agent types or strategies in a single system, often bringing together the best features of each. Imagine if you could take a simple reflex agent (quick decisions), pair it with a model-based agent (a little more thought-out), and throw in some learning capabilities (so the agent keeps improving), and voilà—you've got yourself a hybrid agent.

Now, why would you need a hybrid agent in the first place? Good question! The world is complex, and real-world problems are rarely simple enough to be solved by a single strategy or agent type. By mixing and matching different architectures, you get a system that can handle different situations with more flexibility and adaptability. It's like assembling a super team of agents, each bringing its own skill set to the table to solve a variety of problems. The result? More robust, efficient, and adaptable agents that can thrive in unpredictable and dynamic environments.

What are Hybrid Architectures?

In the world of AI, hybrid architectures refer to a combination of multiple agent models or components working together to solve a task. The idea is that by combining strengths from different approaches, you can create a more powerful, versatile system than what you could achieve with any single model on its own.

Here's an example: Suppose you have a robot trying to navigate an unknown building. A reflex agent could help the robot react to immediate obstacles in its path (quick decisions), while a model-based agent might help it keep track of the layout of the building (a little more thought-out). Combine these with a learning component, and the robot can improve its navigation strategy over time as it learns from its environment. Suddenly, it's not just reacting to obstacles—it's adapting, learning, and getting better with each step.

In essence, hybrid architectures leverage the best of both worlds—combining reactive, pre-programmed rules with more sophisticated, adaptive learning systems to ensure that an AI agent can handle a range of challenges with ease.

The Key Components of Hybrid Architectures

There are a few core strategies that make hybrid architectures so effective:

Combining Reactive and Deliberative Components:

Some hybrid systems combine reactive agents (which act on the spot based on stimuli) with more deliberative agents (which plan ahead and make thoughtful decisions). By using reactive systems for immediate, quick decisions and deliberative systems for complex, long-term planning, hybrid agents can function more effectively in dynamic, real-time environments.

Example: In a self-driving car, the system could use reactive components for immediate actions like emergency braking, while deliberative components plan the route, anticipate traffic conditions, and optimize fuel efficiency.

Combining Rule-Based and Learning-Based Approaches:

One of the most common hybrid architectures is the combination of rule-based systems (where the agent follows a predefined set of rules or logic) with learning-based systems (where the agent learns from experience, such as through reinforcement learning). The rule-based system handles well-understood tasks with clear logic, while the learning-based component adapts and improves performance over time.

Example: A customer service chatbot could use a rule-based system to handle simple inquiries (like providing hours of operation) but switch to a learning-based system to handle more complex queries, adapting its responses based on past interactions.

Combining Multiple Learning Strategies:

Another approach is to combine different types of learning strategies, such as supervised, unsupervised, and reinforcement learning. By leveraging multiple types of learning, hybrid architectures can handle diverse tasks, from pattern recognition to decision-making.

Example: In a recommendation system for streaming services, the AI might use supervised learning to predict preferences based on past user ratings, unsupervised learning to identify new trends and cluster content types, and reinforcement learning to continuously improve recommendations as the user interacts with the system.

Use Cases for Hybrid Architectures

Now that we know how hybrid architectures work, let's talk about some real-world applications that benefit from this flexibility.

Autonomous Vehicles

Self-driving cars are complex systems that require the integration of various agents and technologies. Hybrid architectures are ideal here because autonomous vehicles need to react quickly to environmental changes (reactive components) while also planning long-term strategies (deliberative components). For example, a hybrid system might use reactive agents to avoid immediate obstacles, while planning-based agents figure out the best path to take over longer distances, considering things like traffic and road conditions. The learning component continually improves the car's driving strategies over time based on past driving experiences.

Robotics and Automation

In robotics, hybrid systems allow robots to be more versatile and efficient. For example, a service robot in a hospital might use reactive agents for immediate actions (like avoiding obstacles in the hallway), while a deliberative agent helps plan its tasks (like delivering medicine or assisting patients). The learning component can be employed to refine the robot's movements and decision-making over time, allowing it to become more efficient and accurate in carrying out its duties.

Healthcare Diagnosis Systems

In medical diagnosis, a hybrid system could combine a rule-based system (using predefined medical knowledge to identify symptoms and diagnoses) with a learning agent (which continuously improves by learning from patient data and medical outcomes). This combination helps doctors arrive at more accurate diagnoses faster while also allowing the system to adapt to new medical discoveries or evolving patient needs. The rule-based system ensures the AI remains grounded in well-established medical practices, while the learning component allows the system to stay up-to-date.

Smart Homes

In smart home environments, a hybrid architecture can be used to coordinate different devices and make decisions about energy consumption, security, and comfort. For example, a reactive component might immediately adjust the thermostat when the temperature changes, while a deliberative component plans long-term energy-saving strategies based on patterns of usage over time. A learning component could be added to improve efficiency and anticipate the preferences of the inhabitants, such as adjusting lighting based on when people are usually home or learning which music to play in the morning.

Benefits of Hybrid Architectures

Flexibility: By combining different agents, hybrid systems can adapt to a variety of environments and handle both simple and complex tasks.

Improved Performance: By incorporating multiple types of agents, hybrid systems can benefit from both speed and intelligence, making them faster and more accurate.

Resilience: Hybrid architectures are more robust since they can fall back on simpler agents when the environment becomes too complex, or use more advanced components when needed. This adaptability ensures better performance across a range of scenarios.

Scalability: With hybrid systems, it's easier to scale up a solution. As the system faces more challenges, it can incorporate additional learning and planning components to keep improving.

Conclusion: The Hybrid Future of AI

In the world of AI, hybrid architectures are where the magic happens. By combining the strengths of multiple types of agents and strategies, hybrid systems can address complex, real-world challenges more effectively than any single approach could. The beauty of hybrid systems lies in their flexibility, adaptability, and efficiency, making them a go-to solution for many industries. Whether you're designing a self-driving car or a smart home assistant, hybrid architectures offer a way to optimize performance and improve adaptability. So, next time you see a super-smart AI system, remember—it probably owes its brilliance to a good mix of agents working together.

Chapter 4: Intelligent Behavior and Rationality

Ever wondered what separates a smart agent from one that just looks smart because it guessed correctly? Yeah, us too. This chapter dives into the deep, philosophical swamp of intelligence, where we ask the big questions: Is it smart if it cheats? Is it rational if it ignores obvious solutions? And what happens when an agent optimizes for "efficiency" but forgets not to microwave metal?

This chapter formally explores what constitutes intelligence in artificial agents. It differentiates between rational and irrational behaviors, and introduces the concept of bounded rationality—where agents operate under real-world limitations like incomplete data or limited computation. We also examine how to evaluate agent performance and explore ethical considerations, such as unintended bias in decision-making systems.

4.1 What Constitutes Intelligence in an Agent?

Alright, let's dive into something that's a bit of a brain teaser—what does it actually mean for an agent to be "intelligent"? Now, I know what you're probably thinking: "Isn't intelligence just about knowing stuff, like the walking encyclopedia in your friend group?" Well, sort of. But when it comes to AI agents, intelligence isn't just about having all the facts in your back pocket. It's about being able to reason, adapt, decide, and even learn from mistakes. Think of it like this: if your AI agent were a person, it would need to have a blend of smarts and street-smarts to navigate the complex world around it.

You see, when we think of intelligence, we're usually stuck with an overly simplistic view of IQ tests and memorizing trivia (which, by the way, most humans fail at after one too many drinks). But for AI agents, intelligence means the ability to understand and respond to an environment in a way that's both appropriate and effective. It's more about what an agent does with the information it has and how well it can adjust its approach when things get tough. In other words, we're not just talking about a mind that holds information; we're talking about one that can use it to achieve its goals in unpredictable, dynamic environments. A truly intelligent agent isn't about knowing everything—it's about figuring things out and doing something useful with that knowledge.

Defining Intelligence in AI

In the field of AI, the concept of intelligence is often tied to how well an agent can achieve its goals in a given environment. This ability doesn't simply rely on knowledge but also on the agent's capacity to reason, plan, learn, and adapt. Let's break it down.

Perception and Environment Awareness:

First things first, an intelligent agent needs to be able to perceive its environment. This means having the ability to gather information from its surroundings, process that information, and use it to make informed decisions. This isn't just about being able to "see" or "hear," but rather about interpreting sensory input in a meaningful way. The agent must be able to understand its environment to react appropriately and plan ahead. For example, a self-driving car needs to perceive the road, the vehicles around it, traffic signals, and obstacles, all in real time.

Reasoning and Decision-Making:

Intelligence also involves the ability to reason about the world. This could be in the form of logic (deductive reasoning) or more complex probabilistic reasoning (where the agent has to deal with uncertainty and incomplete information). It means using available knowledge to make sound decisions. A chess-playing AI is a great example of reasoning in action—its intelligence lies in how it decides the best moves based on the current board configuration, past games, and predicted moves of the opponent.

Learning and Adaptation:

Intelligence in AI agents is also about learning from their experiences. This is where things get interesting. A truly intelligent agent doesn't just follow a pre-programmed script; it learns from the environment, adapts its strategies, and improves its performance over time. Reinforcement learning, for example, is an area where agents learn by trial and error, receiving feedback and adjusting their actions accordingly. This learning process allows agents to adapt to new situations and become more efficient in their tasks as they accumulate experience.

Autonomy and Goal-Directed Behavior:

Another key factor in AI intelligence is autonomy—the agent's ability to act on its own, without constant human intervention. Intelligent agents are typically goal-oriented; they can plan and execute a sequence of actions that lead to achieving a specific goal. For instance, a robot vacuum cleaner doesn't need constant guidance; it can autonomously navigate a room, avoid obstacles, and clean efficiently by itself. Its intelligence lies in how it decides the best course of action to achieve the goal of cleaning the room.

Handling Uncertainty and Ambiguity:

Let's face it, life is unpredictable. No one knows exactly what's going to happen next, and that's especially true in dynamic environments. For an AI agent to be truly intelligent, it must handle uncertainty and ambiguity effectively. This is where things get a little more sophisticated. Rather than assuming the world is always clear-cut, intelligent agents must reason under conditions of uncertainty (for example, what happens if the weather forecast changes while you're trying to drive to work?). An agent that can adapt in situations where information is incomplete or noisy (hello, real-world data!) is considered more intelligent than one that fails when things go off-script.

Social Intelligence:

As AI continues to evolve, social intelligence is becoming a crucial element. It's not just about interacting with people, but about understanding social cues, cooperation, and negotiation. Human-robot interaction is one area where social intelligence plays a huge role. A personal assistant AI, for instance, needs to understand the user's preferences, be polite, and adapt to how the user interacts with it. It's about knowing when to be helpful and when to get out of the way. So, in a sense, an intelligent agent also needs to be socially aware in its environment.

Measuring Intelligence: Performance Metrics

We all love a good test, right? Well, in the AI world, there are performance metrics that help determine how intelligent an agent is. These metrics vary depending on the context, but here are a few examples:

Efficiency: How quickly and effectively can the agent achieve its goal? For example, a robot cleaning the floor should aim to clean as much area as possible in the shortest amount of time.

Adaptability: Can the agent learn from its environment and adjust its behavior accordingly? If a chatbot can improve its answers over time based on user feedback, that's adaptability in action.

Accuracy: How well does the agent's decision align with the ideal outcome? In a medical diagnosis system, an accurate diagnosis is a key indicator of intelligence.

Autonomy: To what extent can the agent act independently? A truly intelligent agent can make decisions without human guidance.

Robustness: How well can the agent handle unexpected changes in its environment? A robust agent is one that can continue to perform well even if the environment is unpredictable.

Conclusion: Intelligence is More Than Just Smart Algorithms

To wrap it up, intelligence in AI agents isn't a one-size-fits-all definition. It's about the ability to perceive, reason, learn, and adapt to a constantly changing world. And while algorithms are important, it's the combination of these abilities that creates the intelligent behavior we often see in AI. An agent that can learn from its mistakes, improve over time, and make decisions autonomously is much closer to the intelligent systems we hope to build.

So, next time you hear the term "AI agent," don't just think of a machine following orders. Instead, think of it as a dynamic, adaptive problem-solver—a little like a robot with a sense of direction (and maybe even a good sense of humor, if we get lucky).

4.2 Rational vs. Irrational Behaviors

Let's kick things off with a classic question: What's the difference between rational and irrational behavior? If you're imagining an agent flipping a coin every time it needs to make a decision, you're definitely onto something, but we're aiming for a bit more sophistication here. Rational behavior, in the context of an AI agent, means making decisions that maximize its chances of achieving its goals. Irrational behavior, on the other hand, is when an agent makes decisions that seem to go against its own objectives or act unpredictably in a way that doesn't benefit its long-term success. Think of it as the difference between a smart, calculated decision and an agent having a moment where it's like, "Hey, let's just wing it!"

Now, you might be wondering, "Isn't AI supposed to be all about rationality?" Well, yes, in theory. But let me tell you—even AI agents can be a little bit wild sometimes. After all, they're programmed to make the best possible decisions based on their environment, but if their design is flawed, or if they're working with incomplete or biased information, they can act in ways that seem completely irrational. We might even get a little chuckle from the chaos that ensues. But hey, we can't blame them entirely—it's all about how well they can process the data they've been given and use that info to guide their actions. When they miss the mark? That's when we've got irrational behavior.

Defining Rational Behavior in AI

In the context of AI, rational behavior is defined as any action or decision that maximizes the likelihood of achieving the agent's specific goal. In simple terms, an agent is acting rationally if it is doing the best possible thing it can do to reach its target, given the current information and environment. Rational behavior means an agent is always trying to make the most optimal decisions based on the conditions it faces.

The key here is goal achievement—the agent must act in a way that directly contributes to meeting its predefined goal. This isn't necessarily about acting in a "perfect" or "flawless" way, but about making choices that are logically aligned with its goals, based on the information it has.

For example, a self-driving car is designed to safely and efficiently reach a destination. It is constantly receiving data from its sensors and environment, such as road conditions, traffic, obstacles, and other cars. Based on this data, the car's decisions—whether it's adjusting its speed, braking, or turning—are all made with one goal in mind: to drive safely and efficiently to its destination. If it decides to slow down at a traffic light rather than speeding through, it's acting rationally because that decision minimizes the risk of an accident and ultimately helps the car achieve its goal.

However, rational behavior can also be somewhat context-dependent. What's rational in one situation might not be rational in another. In the case of an AI agent, rationality is typically defined relative to the agent's goals and environment.

What Makes an AI Agent Irrational?

If rational behavior is about achieving goals efficiently and effectively, then irrational behavior is any action or decision that is either:

Suboptimal or

Directly counterproductive to achieving the agent's goals.

Irrationality often arises when an agent either:

Misunderstands the environment, causing it to act in ways that are misaligned with its goals,

Lacks sufficient information to make an informed decision (leading it to make guesswork-based decisions), or

Uses flawed algorithms that lead it to make decisions that seem weird, illogical, or downright nonsensical.

Let's take an example. Imagine an autonomous robot vacuum that's programmed to clean the house. Rational behavior would be for the robot to systematically move around the room, avoiding obstacles and covering as much of the floor as possible. However, if the robot randomly zooms to one corner of the room, spins in circles, and then gets stuck under the couch, that's clearly irrational behavior. The robot isn't achieving its cleaning goal in the most efficient way. It might be facing obstacles, but it's failing to adapt and make smarter decisions. It's acting like a toddler who doesn't understand the point of cleaning—they're just doing stuff without really thinking it through.

Irrational behavior in AI agents can stem from many things—poorly designed algorithms, inaccurate sensors, or even insufficient data. If the agent doesn't have all the information it needs to make an informed decision, it might make choices that appear out of left field. Similarly, an agent's learning process might result in irrational decisions if it doesn't have a proper feedback mechanism. For instance, a reinforcement learning agent might over-prioritize short-term rewards and ignore long-term goals, leading to seemingly irrational behavior.

Rationality vs. Perfection

Now, let's take a quick detour to talk about an important distinction—rationality isn't the same as perfection. An AI agent can be rational without making every decision perfectly. In fact, many rational agents are designed to make trade-offs between competing factors (e.g., speed vs. safety, accuracy vs. efficiency).

Take a delivery drone, for instance. The rational behavior for the drone might be to deliver a package as quickly as possible. However, this could mean that the drone will need to make decisions such as avoiding weather conditions or taking a longer, safer route to avoid bad air conditions. The drone might not make the fastest decision every time, but it's still being rational because it's balancing priorities and acting in a way that minimizes the risk of failure.

In contrast, irrational behavior would be if the drone decides to take the most dangerous, direct route, despite clear warnings from its sensors about poor weather. That would be an agent acting against its goal of safe delivery, putting it at risk and potentially harming itself and its package.

The Role of Uncertainty in Rationality

A big reason why AI agents might appear irrational is because they have to make decisions under conditions of uncertainty. In the real world, information is rarely perfect, and agents are often faced with incomplete data. The key for rational agents is how they handle uncertainty.

For example, consider a weather prediction AI. The rational behavior of this agent is to make the best possible forecast based on available data. However, if the data is incomplete or conflicting (say, a sudden temperature spike in a previously stable environment), the agent might make a prediction that isn't entirely accurate. But in a world filled with uncertainty, the fact that it made a decision based on available data doesn't make it irrational. It's simply acting within the limitations of its environment. On the other hand, if the agent simply ignores the available data or makes a wild guess, that would be irrational.

Conclusion: Rationality is About Effective Goal Achievement

In the end, the difference between rational and irrational behavior in AI agents comes down to how effectively they achieve their goals. A rational agent carefully assesses the environment, reasons through options, and takes the most effective course of action based on the information it has. On the flip side, irrational behavior happens when an agent makes decisions that do not lead to goal achievement or are counterproductive to its objectives. It's not always about perfection—it's about making decisions that are logically aligned with the agent's goals and working with what's available.

So, next time your AI agent seems a little confused or unpredictable, just remember: it's not just randomly "winging it" (well, at least, we hope it's not). It's probably facing some uncertainty or lack of information, but that's all part of the fun journey of AI!

4.3 Bounded Rationality and Real-World Constraints

Alright, here's the thing about rationality: in theory, an agent should make the best possible decision based on all available information and in pursuit of its goal. But guess what? The world isn't always so neat and tidy, and neither are the agents we build. Enter the concept of bounded rationality—the idea that even the smartest AI agents are limited in how rational they can be because they're working with imperfect information, limited resources, and time constraints. It's like trying to solve a puzzle with half the pieces missing, while someone is constantly yelling at you to hurry up. The result? Well, let's just say the puzzle might not look perfect when you're done, but it'll be the best you can do under the circumstances.

The truth is, no AI agent operates in a vacuum with endless data and perfect conditions. Real-world environments are messy, unpredictable, and constantly changing. Think about how even the most advanced AI systems (like your virtual assistant or self-driving car) can still run into problems that make them seem less than "intelligent." They're doing the best they can with what they have, but their ability to be perfectly rational is constrained by the limitations they face. Bounded rationality acknowledges this and tells us that perfect decision-making is often out of reach—and that's okay. Sometimes, "good enough" is actually the most rational choice an agent can make.

What Is Bounded Rationality?

The concept of bounded rationality was first introduced by Nobel laureate Herbert Simon in 1957. Simon suggested that while humans (and by extension, AI agents) try to make rational decisions, their ability to do so is limited by the information they have, their computational power, and the time they can afford to make decisions. Instead of striving for an optimal solution, bounded rationality suggests that agents often settle for a satisficing solution—one that is good enough, even if it's not the absolute best possible choice.

In practical terms, this means that AI agents are often forced to make decisions within the limits of their environment and available data. Let's be honest: if an agent had to run through every possible scenario before making a move, it would take forever and probably never get anything done. The solution? Shortcuts—like approximations, heuristics, or simplified models that allow agents to make decisions quickly and effectively, even if they don't have all the information they ideally would need.

For example, imagine a delivery drone that has to choose between two possible routes to reach a destination. The ideal solution might involve evaluating every possible route and considering traffic conditions, wind speed, obstacles, and a host of other factors. But, given limited time and resources, the drone might just rely on a heuristic—say, taking the route with the least congestion based on past data—and making an educated guess about how much time it will save. In this case, the drone is using bounded rationality—it's not optimizing for every possible variable, but instead choosing a good-enough solution that allows it to get the job done in a timely manner.

Real-World Constraints on AI Agents

The reason why bounded rationality is such a crucial concept in AI development is that agents almost never have access to perfect information. In the real world, we're dealing with constraints that can affect an agent's decision-making ability in several ways. Let's break down some of these constraints and how they limit rationality:

Incomplete Information:

In the real world, AI agents rarely have access to all the data they would need to make a truly rational decision. A self-driving car, for example, can't know what every driver on the road is thinking or how the weather might change in the next few minutes. This makes it difficult for the car to make the "perfect" decision at every moment. Instead, it needs to make decisions based on limited information, and sometimes, those decisions are less than optimal but still good enough to keep the car moving safely.

Time Constraints:

Another big factor in bounded rationality is time. We all know that in the real world, there's often little time to deliberate over every single decision. In many situations, AI agents have to make decisions in real-time, which means they can't afford to run through every possible solution before acting. A robotic surgery system, for instance, may have only milliseconds to make decisions based on sensor data during an operation. In these situations, agents use approximations and fast heuristics to make the best decision in the time available, even if it's not the absolute optimal choice.

Computational Power:

AI agents are often limited by the computational resources they have at their disposal. A complex, resource-heavy decision-making process might be out of reach for an agent if it doesn't have enough processing power. This is especially true for devices like smartphones or edge devices that can't afford to do massive calculations all the time. So instead, agents use simplified models that allow them to make decisions with the limited computational power they have. This again leads to bounded rationality, where agents have to settle for "good enough" solutions based on their computational limits.

Environmental Uncertainty:

The world is unpredictable. Weather changes, traffic jams, human behavior—all of these factors introduce uncertainty into an agent's environment. In order to make decisions under such uncertain conditions, agents rely on probabilistic reasoning or risk assessments. These tools help agents predict what's most likely to happen, even if they don't have all the details. For example, a stock trading agent might analyze market trends and make predictions, but there's always uncertainty involved because no model can fully predict human behavior or sudden market shifts.

How AI Agents Deal with Bounded Rationality

So how do AI agents cope with bounded rationality? Well, they employ a combination of heuristics, approximations, and real-time decision-making strategies to make the best possible choice within their constraints.

Heuristics:

These are shortcuts or rules of thumb that help AI agents make decisions without needing to analyze every piece of information. Think of it like a quick-and-dirty strategy that works most of the time, but isn't guaranteed to be perfect. For example, in a navigation system, an agent might use the shortest path algorithm as a heuristic, rather than considering every possible route in detail.

Approximations:

AI agents often rely on approximating the ideal solution, especially in complex environments where exact answers aren't feasible. For example, a recommendation engine might not know exactly what you want, but it can approximate your preferences based on past behavior or similar users.

Learning and Adaptation:

Agents can learn from experience and adapt their behavior over time to improve their decision-making process under real-world constraints. For example, a smart home system might learn from your behavior patterns and adjust its thermostat settings accordingly, even though it doesn't have full information about your preferences.

Conclusion: "Good Enough" Can Be Really Good

At the end of the day, bounded rationality is all about recognizing that perfection is out of reach. AI agents are not superhumans with infinite processing power and access to infinite data. Instead, they have to make the best decisions they can with the time, information, and resources available to them. The goal isn't to be perfect, it's to be effective—and in the real world, that often means choosing a "good enough" solution that gets the job done, rather than obsessing over an ideal one. So, the next time your AI agent doesn't seem to have it all together, just remember: it's still doing its best within the constraints it has. And honestly, isn't that what we all do every day?

4.4 Measuring Agent Performance

Here's the thing about AI agents: just like us, they can't really improve without a little feedback. How do you know if your AI is any good at its job? Well, unlike the mysterious way your office printer works (and definitely better than that), we have a straightforward way to figure out if your AI agent is performing like a rockstar or just stumbling around like a toddler in a new pair of shoes. Performance metrics are the key to understanding how well an agent is doing. But here's where it gets interesting—performance isn't always about winning, being perfect, or finishing first. It's about achieving goals efficiently, effectively, and without causing unnecessary chaos (though, let's be honest, a little chaos makes things fun sometimes, right?).

To get a handle on this, we need to define measurable goals. Whether we're talking about a self-driving car, a robotic vacuum, or even an AI chess-playing agent, we need to ask: "Is it doing what it's supposed to do, and is it doing it well?" How do we know? It all comes down to quantifiable metrics that let us track its success rate, efficiency, and accuracy. But don't worry, we won't get too deep into technical jargon. Instead, I'll break it down and make it clear why measuring AI performance matters, and how you can know when your agents are truly working at their best (or need a little TLC).

The Basics: What to Measure in Agent Performance

When we talk about measuring agent performance, we're essentially asking, "How do we know if the agent is doing its job properly?" Well, it's not a single number or simple answer. Performance varies depending on what the agent is designed to do. But to keep it simple, let's break it down into three main criteria that usually apply across the board:

Goal Achievement

The most obvious metric to consider is whether the agent is achieving its goals. If the goal of the agent is to clean your house (looking at you, robot vacuum), then its performance can be measured by how well it covers the floor, avoids obstacles, and doesn't get stuck under the couch. If it finishes the job and doesn't miss spots, you can say, "Good job, vacuum!" Similarly, for a self-driving car, the goal is usually to reach a destination safely and efficiently. If the car avoids obstacles, follows traffic laws, and safely arrives at the destination, that's a performance win.

But of course, goal achievement alone doesn't paint the whole picture. For instance, a drone might successfully deliver a package, but if it crashes halfway through, we've got a serious problem. So, we need to think about how the agent meets its goal efficiently.

Efficiency

Efficiency is about how well an agent performs its tasks, and it's often measured by time, energy, or resources consumed. For example, when measuring the performance of a recommendation system, you might want to know how quickly it can analyze customer preferences and generate suggestions. If the system takes too long, then it's not very efficient, no matter how accurate the recommendations are.

For a robotic arm in manufacturing, efficiency could be about how many parts it can assemble per minute. The faster it completes its task without errors, the more efficient it is. In contrast, if the robot takes forever to assemble something and makes multiple mistakes, then it's performing inefficiently, even if it eventually finishes.

Accuracy

The third criterion we'll talk about is accuracy. This refers to how precise an agent's actions or decisions are. An AI agent might meet its goals and do it relatively quickly, but if it's inaccurate, it's like building a house with uneven walls—sure, it's technically a house, but nobody wants to live in it. For instance, a predictive model used in finance might aim to predict market trends. If the model's predictions are mostly wrong, it's inaccurate, no matter how fast or efficiently it operates.

In a self-driving car, accuracy would mean making the right decisions about speed, steering, and avoiding obstacles in real-time. A small mistake in judgment could result in a crash, so accuracy is critical here. Measuring accuracy allows us to determine if an agent is making the right decisions at the right time, given its goals and environment.

Specific Performance Metrics for Different Agents

Now that we know the broad categories, let's dive into a few real-world examples of how performance metrics are applied to specific AI agents.

Self-Driving Cars:

For autonomous vehicles, there are a ton of metrics to consider. Some common ones include:

Distance traveled without incidents: How far the car can drive without getting into an accident or making a mistake (such as running a red light or cutting off another vehicle).

Time to destination: How quickly the car reaches its destination, while maintaining safety and following traffic laws.

Accuracy of route planning: How well the car can predict and adjust its route based on real-time traffic conditions.

Chatbots and Virtual Assistants:

A virtual assistant, like Siri or Alexa, can be evaluated based on:

Response accuracy: Does it provide correct answers or perform the requested task correctly?

Response time: How fast does it respond to queries?

User satisfaction: How happy are users with the assistant's responses?

Robotic Systems:

When we evaluate robots, whether it's a factory robot or a robotic vacuum, the performance metrics often include:

Task completion rate: Did the robot complete its assigned task?

Error rate: Did it make mistakes, such as dropping parts or failing to clean a section?

Resource consumption: How much energy or material did the robot use in the process?

Trade-offs in Measuring Performance

Here's the thing—measuring agent performance is not always as clear-cut as you might think. Sometimes, improving one metric can negatively affect another. For example, a delivery drone might be able to reach its destination more quickly by flying in a straight line, but this could increase the risk of running into obstacles, reducing accuracy or safety. Similarly, a recommendation engine might increase its accuracy by processing a massive amount of data, but that might slow down its response time. So, it's crucial to consider how different performance measures interact and affect one another.

At the end of the day, balancing multiple performance metrics is what really helps us understand how well an agent is doing. It's about making trade-offs and optimizing performance across various criteria to ensure that the agent meets its goals in the best possible way.

Conclusion: Performance Is More Than Just the Result

In conclusion, measuring AI agent performance is a mix of art and science. Sure, you want to know if your agent can achieve its goal, but you also want to know if it's doing so in an efficient and accurate way. The more metrics you have, the clearer picture you get of the agent's overall success. And remember, good performance is all about balance. Sometimes you have to sacrifice a little efficiency for better accuracy, or vice versa. The goal is to find the sweet spot where the agent is performing optimally, given the constraints it faces.

So, the next time you interact with an AI agent, take a moment to appreciate the balance of goals, efficiency, and accuracy at play. And remember, even if it's not perfect, as long as it's doing the job, it's a job well done in the world of AI!

4.5 Ethical Considerations and Bias in AI Agents

Let's talk about something that's often left out of the glamorous "AI revolution" hype: ethics. Sure, AI agents are cool. They're smart. They're efficient. But have you ever stopped to think about the ethics behind how they make decisions, or how those decisions might affect us? AI is not just about cold, hard logic and mathematical models; it's about people, society, and trust. Imagine this: you're on the receiving end of an AI hiring tool that makes a decision about whether you get an interview for your dream job. Now imagine that the AI has been trained on biased data from past hiring decisions, and suddenly, you find out that the system doesn't seem too keen on hiring people with certain characteristics. Uh-oh. Now we've got a problem, haven't we?

The truth is, ethical considerations in AI aren't just a nice-to-have—they're a must-have. Whether it's data privacy, decision transparency, or accountability for AI-driven decisions, we need to ensure that the technology we build aligns with our values and doesn't cause harm. This subchapter will tackle some of the most pressing ethical questions about AI agents and explore the growing concern of bias in AI decision-making. Don't worry, I'm not going to be all doom and gloom about this, but we can't ignore the fact that AI's influence on our lives needs to be handled with care. If we're going to live in a world full of intelligent agents, it's time to make sure those agents play nice.

The Ethical Dilemma of AI: Who's in Charge?

First things first: who decides what's ethical for an AI agent? The answer is… it's complicated. In theory, the creators of AI systems are the ones who get to set the ethical standards. But here's the twist—AI agents are increasingly making decisions without direct human intervention. So, how do we ensure that the AI isn't making decisions that conflict with our values or rights?

One of the biggest challenges in AI ethics is the concept of accountability. When an AI agent makes a decision that harms someone, who is responsible? If a self-driving car makes a mistake and causes an accident, who takes the fall—the car manufacturer, the AI developer, or the car itself? As AI systems become more autonomous, the question of accountability becomes even more critical. We need laws, regulations, and clear frameworks to determine who is held responsible for the actions of AI agents.

Take, for example, AI in healthcare. AI systems can assist in diagnosing diseases, suggesting treatment options, and even performing surgeries. These systems are often built to be autonomous and can make high-stakes decisions based on the data they're given. But if the AI makes a mistake—say, misdiagnoses a condition—who's liable? The developer? The healthcare provider using the system? The AI itself? The issue of accountability is thorny, and it's something we'll have to figure out as AI continues to evolve.

Bias in AI: When Machines Learn the Wrong Lessons

One of the most dangerous ethical issues in AI today is bias. And no, I'm not talking about the fact that your AI assistant seems to know exactly when you're running low on coffee (but hey, that's impressive!). I'm talking about the systemic bias that can creep into AI systems when they're trained on biased data. Here's how it works: AI agents learn from the data they're fed, and if that data reflects human prejudices—well, the AI can pick up on that, too. And the problem is, these biased AI systems can perpetuate discrimination on a massive scale.

For instance, if an AI system is trained to evaluate job applicants based on resumes, but the training data comes from historical hiring practices where certain demographics were unfairly overlooked, the AI might "learn" that people from those demographics are less qualified—when, in reality, that's not true at all. This is a form of algorithmic bias that can have serious consequences, leading to decisions that harm underrepresented groups, perpetuate inequality, and even create a vicious cycle of exclusion.

This isn't just theoretical, either. Bias in AI is already affecting real-world systems. From facial recognition technology that struggles to accurately identify people with darker skin tones, to criminal justice algorithms that unfairly target minority communities, AI bias has been linked to some pretty troubling outcomes. The reality is that AI is only as good as the data it learns from—and if that data reflects human bias, well, the AI will reflect those biases too.

Tackling Bias: Can We Fix It?

Now that we know how bias can sneak into AI, the big question is—can we fix it? The answer is yes, but it's a work in progress. One way to address bias is by being more mindful during the data collection process. AI developers need to ensure that the data used to train AI systems is diverse, representative, and free from historical biases. It's also essential to regularly audit AI systems for bias and adjust their training data when issues are discovered.

Another way to combat bias is by developing fairness-aware algorithms. These algorithms are designed to detect and reduce bias during the decision-making process. For example, fairness constraints can be built into AI models, ensuring that they don't discriminate based on sensitive attributes like race, gender, or age. But creating truly fair AI is tough—because fairness itself is a subjective concept. What's fair to one person might not be fair to another, so defining and enforcing fairness in AI systems is a continuous challenge.

It's also worth noting that human oversight is crucial when it comes to combating bias. AI shouldn't be left entirely to its own devices, especially in high-stakes decisions like hiring, law enforcement, or healthcare. Humans need to be involved in the process, ensuring that the decisions made by AI agents align with human values and ethical standards. After all, AI may be smart, but it's not a replacement for human judgment—especially when it comes to matters of fairness and ethics.

Privacy: Who Owns Your Data?

Speaking of humans, privacy is another ethical consideration we can't ignore. AI agents often need access to personal data to function—whether it's for making recommendations, analyzing patterns, or driving autonomous vehicles. But that data comes with responsibilities. Who owns that data? Should AI systems be allowed to collect and use it without explicit consent? What happens if that data is misused or falls into the wrong hands?

The ethical dilemma around data privacy is that, on one hand, AI systems often need personal data to function optimally. But on the other hand, users should have control over their own data and how it's used. Transparency is key here—AI developers must be upfront about what data they're collecting, how it's being used, and who has access to it. Users should be able to make informed decisions about what data they're willing to share, and AI systems should respect their privacy preferences.

Conclusion: Building Ethical AI for a Better Future

At the end of the day, ethics isn't just an afterthought in AI development—it's essential. We need to ensure that AI agents are designed to align with our moral values, respect human rights, and act responsibly. From tackling bias to ensuring accountability, transparency, and fairness, there's a lot to consider when building AI systems that are not just intelligent, but also ethical. The future of AI depends on responsible development and ongoing dialogue about how we want these agents to interact with the world.

So, the next time you ask Siri to play your favorite song, or interact with a chatbot, remember: there's more than meets the eye. AI is not just about algorithms and data—it's about making sure these agents work for us, without causing harm or reinforcing inequality. After all, we're in the driver's seat here, and we've got the ethical compass to steer this AI revolution in the right direction.

Chapter 5: Agent Architectures

Designing an AI agent is like building a burrito—you can go with simple ingredients (reflexes), pack in some thoughtful layering (deliberation), or combine it all in a glorious hybrid monster that does everything… until it breaks. In this chapter, we build from the ground up, exploring different ways to stack an agent's brain without causing a software-induced identity crisis.

This chapter introduces the primary architectural paradigms used in AI agent design. We discuss reactive architectures focused on immediate response, deliberative systems that plan actions based on models, and layered architectures that combine both for balance. Additional focus is placed on subsumption and behavior-based approaches, with guidelines for selecting appropriate architectures based on application requirements.

5.1 Reactive Architectures

Imagine you're playing a game of ping-pong. You don't have time to plan your moves in advance. You just react. The ball comes at you, you swing, and you hope you hit it right back. That's essentially how reactive architectures work in AI. They don't have a memory of past events, nor do they have a long-term plan. Instead, they respond immediately to current stimuli in their environment. It's like your AI agent is a reflex machine—no deep thought, no grand strategy, just straight-up reacting to what's in front of it. You could think of them as the AI equivalent of a knee-jerk reaction. It's fast, it's simple, and sometimes, it's surprisingly effective.

But here's the catch: while reactive agents can be super efficient and great for specific tasks, they also lack the fancy decision-making skills you might associate with higher-level AI. You'll never see a reactive agent planning its next move or plotting out how to save the world. It's all about reacting to immediate input. But don't be fooled—there's more to these agents than just "react and repeat." We'll dive into how these systems work, their strengths, and their limitations, and you'll see why they're still an essential part of the AI world.

How Reactive Architectures Work

In a reactive architecture, the agent has no internal model of the world or history of past events. The agent's actions are purely based on the current perception of the environment and the immediate input it receives. No memory, no problem—the agent just does what it needs to do based on the situation right in front of it.

The core idea here is that no internal reasoning is required. A reactive agent simply perceives the environment through sensors, and based on that perception, it executes an action using its actuators. For example, a robot vacuum may detect dirt, and based on that input, it immediately decides to turn on the vacuum and start cleaning. No complex reasoning, no second-guessing—just action. Simple, efficient, and direct.

In a more complex system, a reactive agent could be something like a self-driving car responding to immediate threats—like a car stopping in front of it or a pedestrian crossing the street. The agent would react by applying the brakes or steering to avoid the obstacle. Again, this system doesn't plan its next five moves, but it reacts immediately to the environment in real-time, ensuring safety.

Key Characteristics of Reactive Architectures

Let's break down the major features of reactive architectures to better understand how they work and when they make sense:

Stimulus-Response Mechanism

At the heart of any reactive agent is the stimulus-response model. This means that the agent doesn't spend time thinking about the future or learning from past actions. It just responds to current stimuli from its environment. Imagine a robotic lawnmower that detects grass and starts mowing—its behavior is purely reactionary based on the input from its sensors, like the type of terrain it detects.

No Internal Model of the World

One of the most defining features of reactive agents is that they don't have an internal model or memory of the world. Reactive systems operate solely on real-time sensory data. They don't track their past actions, nor do they anticipate future events. They don't plan or predict—they just react to what's in front of them. This makes them simple, but also limits their ability to make complex decisions over time.

Real-Time Action

Because reactive agents don't have to deal with complicated processing or planning, they can respond in real-time. This makes them incredibly fast and efficient for tasks that don't require long-term planning. Think about a robotic arm on an assembly line. It doesn't have to think about its next move—it reacts to the presence of parts on the conveyor belt, picking them up and moving them exactly where they need to go. It's quick, precise, and doesn't waste time with unnecessary thought.

Advantages of Reactive Architectures

So, what's the big deal with reactive architectures? Why are they so widely used in AI systems today? Well, let me tell you, simplicity is their greatest strength. Reactive agents are straightforward, easy to design, and highly efficient for specific tasks. Here are some reasons why reactive systems can be incredibly useful:

Speed and Efficiency

Because they don't have to waste time with planning or decision-making, reactive agents can respond incredibly fast. For applications that require immediate action, this kind of system can be a lifesaver. Self-driving cars, for example, need to react quickly to road conditions, so a reactive agent can make instant decisions, like braking or steering.

Low Computational Resources

Reactive systems tend to require fewer computational resources than more complex AI agents that rely on internal models or planning. For example, a robotic vacuum cleaner that just cleans up dust in real-time doesn't need complex algorithms or massive data processing power. It just does its thing based on immediate input, making it an affordable and efficient option for many use cases.

Simplicity in Design

Let's face it—sometimes simple is better. Reactive systems are easy to design and implement. There's no need for complex algorithms or massive data sets to train the system. This makes them an attractive choice for applications where straightforward actions based on immediate stimuli are sufficient.

Limitations of Reactive Architectures

While reactive systems have their perks, they're not without limitations. Let's face it—if all your AI agent can do is react to whatever is in front of it, that's a bit like being in a ping-pong match with no strategy. It's quick, but it's not exactly winning any awards for long-term planning or creative problem-solving.

Lack of Long-Term Planning

One of the most significant downsides of reactive architectures is that they don't plan for the future. This means they can't handle tasks that require complex future thinking or goal-based decision-making. For example, a robot may be able to pick up objects and sort them, but it won't have the ability to plan out an entire task and strategize its actions over time.

Inflexibility in Changing Environments

Reactive systems are often rigid because they rely purely on immediate sensory input. If the environment changes in unexpected ways, a reactive agent may struggle to adapt. For instance, a robot programmed to navigate a warehouse might struggle if the layout changes—without a model of the world or the ability to learn, it can't adjust its strategy to new circumstances.

No Learning from Experience

Reactive agents don't "learn" from their experiences. They don't improve over time or adjust their behavior based on past actions. This can make them less adaptable in dynamic, complex environments. Over time, learning-based agents or goal-based agents can become much better at their tasks, but a reactive system will remain stuck in a repetitive loop.

Use Cases for Reactive Architectures

Despite the limitations, reactive architectures are far from obsolete. In fact, they're highly effective in specific use cases where simple, quick reactions are all that's needed. Here are a few examples:

Autonomous Vehicles: While fully autonomous vehicles rely on complex planning and decision-making, some aspects of the car's behavior, like collision avoidance, are purely reactive.

Robotic Vacuum Cleaners: These robots don't need a complex plan for cleaning your house. They detect dirt, and based on that, they start cleaning. Simple as that.

Industrial Automation: Robotic arms and conveyor belts work by reacting to the immediate needs of the assembly line without any need for deep analysis or planning.

Conclusion: The Power of Simplicity

In the world of AI, reactive architectures are the MVPs for tasks that require speed and efficiency. These systems don't overthink—they just act. And sometimes, that's all you need. But remember, while reactive agents are great for certain tasks, they're not the answer for everything. They lack planning and adaptability, and they can't handle complex, evolving problems. So, when designing your AI agent, ask yourself: Do I need a genius with a plan, or just a fast and reliable responder? The answer might be simpler than you think.

5.2 Deliberative Architectures

Alright, picture this: you're at an ice cream shop with twenty flavors staring you in the face. Do you immediately pick chocolate because it's safe and reliable (like a reactive agent)? Or do you stand there, paralyzed by choice, mentally simulating every taste combination to maximize your ice cream happiness? If you're the latter, congrats—you think like a deliberative agent. Unlike their reactive cousins, deliberative architectures take their sweet time. They plan, reason, predict, and analyze before they act. They build an internal model of the world, simulate possible futures, and then choose the best action. In short, they're the strategists of the AI world.

While this sounds all glamorous and Nobel-Prize-worthy, deliberative agents have their own headaches: they're slower, heavier on computation, and sometimes struggle in environments where split-second decisions are critical. But for complex, multi-step goals where the wrong move could spell disaster (looking at you, Mars rovers), deliberative thinking is not just handy—it's essential.

How Deliberative Architectures Work

Deliberative architectures are based on the classic sense-think-act cycle.

Here's how it rolls:

Sense: Gather information about the environment through sensors.

Think: Build or update an internal model of the world.

Act: Plan a course of action based on goals, constraints, and predictions.

Unlike reactive agents who just act immediately based on stimuli, deliberative agents pause to think. They ponder their options. They simulate the consequences of different actions using their internal model before committing to anything. This gives them a huge advantage in complex environments where simple reactions just won't cut it.

For example, if you're designing a robot to navigate a maze, a reactive agent might bounce around blindly hoping to find the exit. A deliberative agent, however, would map out the maze, plan a path to the goal, and execute that path step-by-step, adjusting if new obstacles arise.

Key Characteristics of Deliberative Architectures

Let's unpack the defining traits of these slow-but-smart AI agents:

Internal World Model

Deliberative agents maintain an internal representation of their environment. This model is continuously updated based on new sensory input. It's like they have a mental map of the world they're navigating.

Planning and Reasoning

They don't just react; they plan. This involves setting goals, considering multiple action sequences, predicting outcomes, and selecting the most appropriate course of action. Think of it like playing chess—considering multiple future moves before making your next one.

Goal-Oriented Behavior

Every action the agent takes is designed to achieve specific goals. They don't just randomly act—they act with purpose, even if that means waiting, detouring, or making compromises along the way.

Flexibility and Adaptability

When the environment changes, a good deliberative agent doesn't freak out. It updates its world model and replans its actions. This ability to adapt is what makes them so powerful for real-world applications where unpredictability is the norm.

Advantages of Deliberative Architectures

Deliberative systems may be slower than reactive systems, but their depth of reasoning offers massive benefits:

Handling Complexity

These agents shine in complex, dynamic environments where careful planning is needed. They can handle multiple goals, constraints, and unexpected changes with grace.

Efficient Goal Achievement

Deliberative agents don't waste time (in theory) doing useless actions. Their planning process ensures that every step taken contributes meaningfully toward the final objective.

Problem Solving

They can analyze new problems, evaluate different strategies, and make informed decisions rather than reacting blindly. Perfect for tasks like strategic gameplay, space exploration, or autonomous disaster recovery robots.

Limitations of Deliberative Architectures

Of course, nothing's perfect (except maybe coffee and naps), and deliberative architectures come with their own juicy drawbacks:

Computationally Heavy

Maintaining and constantly updating an internal world model, plus running complex planning algorithms, is expensive in terms of computing resources. Not ideal if you're working with limited hardware.

Slower Response Times

In rapidly changing environments where split-second decisions are needed (like avoiding a flying pigeon while driving), deliberative agents might simply be too slow. Sometimes you just need to slam the brakes, not run a 30-step simulation on whether you should.

Model Inaccuracy

If the internal model of the world is wrong or incomplete, the agent's carefully crafted plans can fail spectacularly. Garbage in, garbage out.

Use Cases for Deliberative Architectures

So where does this slow-cooked, highly thought-out approach shine brightest? Glad you asked:

Autonomous Vehicles: Higher-level decision-making like route planning, fuel optimization, and traffic negotiation relies on deliberation.

Space Exploration: Think Mars Rovers planning their paths across tricky Martian terrain without a human joystick.

Service Robots: Robots working in hospitals, hotels, or warehouses where they need to plan deliveries or schedules.

Game AI: Strategic AI opponents that plan their moves ahead (so they can absolutely demolish you in chess).

The Best of Both Worlds: Hybrids

Because the real world is messy, chaotic, and doesn't always play by the rules, most modern AI agents use hybrid architectures—combining reactive and deliberative elements. This gives agents the ability to react quickly when necessary while still planning ahead when time allows.

(Think of it like being able to both dodge a flying football and still keep your eyes on the long-term goal of winning the game.)

Conclusion: Think, Then Act (But Maybe Hurry Up a Bit)

Deliberative architectures are the chess masters, the strategic planners, the deep thinkers of the AI agent universe. They give us agents that don't just react—they reason, plan, and strive toward goals in a smart and calculated way.

Sure, they're not the fastest guns in the West, and sure, sometimes you want to yell at them to hurry up already—but when it comes to tackling complex, long-term problems, you'll want these slow and steady agents on your side.

(And hey, sometimes in life—and in AI—you've got to stop, think, and then sprint blindly into the chaos.)

5.3 Layered Architectures

Imagine you're trying to juggle making breakfast, checking your emails, and dodging your cat, who just decided your kitchen is the new Formula 1 racetrack. If you tried to do all of these at once with a single, linear brain process, you'd probably burn the toast, send an email full of gibberish, and trip over the cat. Instead, what do you do? You layer your priorities: immediate reactions (jump over the cat), short-term plans (make coffee first, then toast), and long-term goals (somehow make it to work before 9 AM).

Congratulations—you just modeled layered architecture in your own brain! And it's exactly this idea that AI architects stole (ahem, borrowed) to design smarter, more adaptable agents.

What Are Layered Architectures?

At its core, a layered architecture breaks an agent's behavior into distinct levels or layers, each responsible for different types of thinking and action.

Each layer deals with a different aspect of the agent's behavior:

The bottom layer handles immediate, reflex-like responses (e.g., "jump over cat").

The middle layers manage routine behaviors and plans (e.g., "prepare breakfast").

The top layers focus on high-level, long-term goals (e.g., "have a productive day").

Each layer operates either independently, in parallel, or in a controlled hierarchy, depending on how the architecture is designed. It's a beautiful, chaotic dance of priorities—and when it works right, it's pure magic.

How Layered Architectures Work

There are typically two ways these layers interact:

Vertical Communication (Hierarchical)

Higher layers issue goals or commands to lower layers. Lower layers act on immediate inputs and report status back up.

Horizontal Communication (Parallel)

Layers operate more or less independently but may share information. If two layers conflict, a conflict resolution mechanism steps in.

Some systems even use a combination of both to balance flexibility with control.

In practice, layered architectures enable agents to simultaneously handle reactive responses and deliberative planning—a massive improvement over single-track agents.

Types of Layered Architectures

There are many flavors of layered architectures (like lasagna types), but a few famous ones include:

Subsumption Architecture (Brooks, 1986)

Lower layers can suppress or subsume higher layers. Very reactive and used in early mobile robotics.

Touring Machines

Mixes reactive, planning, and modeling layers for richer behavior control.

3T (Three-Tier Architecture)

Divides behavior into skill-based reactive, sequencing-based executive, and planning-based deliberative components.

Each model offers different balances between reactivity, planning, and adaptability.

Advantages of Layered Architectures

Why slice an agent into layers? Well:

Flexibility

Agents can respond immediately to dangers (through reactive layers) without waiting for complex planning layers to catch up.

Robustness

If a high-level plan fails, lower layers can still keep the agent alive and kicking.

Scalability

It's easier to add new skills or behaviors by inserting new layers without redesigning the whole system.

Efficiency

Urgent tasks don't clog up cognitive bandwidth intended for bigger picture planning.

Challenges of Layered Architectures

Of course, with great layering comes great... messiness:

Conflict Between Layers

What happens if your reactive layer screams "RUN!" while your planning layer calmly suggests, "Proceed cautiously"? Without good conflict resolution, you get an agent doing the robot equivalent of panic-dancing.

Communication Overhead

More layers mean more coordination. If not designed carefully, this can slow down decision-making or cause "analysis paralysis."

Debugging Complexity

Figuring out why an agent took a bizarre action can be tough when you're dealing with ten different layers influencing behavior.

Real-World Applications

Layered architectures show up wherever you need complex, flexible agents:

Robotics

Robots navigating unfamiliar terrain need quick reactions (avoid obstacles) and thoughtful planning (get to destination safely).

Autonomous Vehicles

Self-driving cars have layers for emergency braking, routine lane-following, and strategic navigation.

Game AI

Characters in video games often use layered systems to blend immediate reactions (duck from gunfire) and longer-term strategy (flank the enemy).

Virtual Assistants

Systems like Siri and Alexa blend instant responses (answer your joke question) with background processes managing tasks and context over time.

Why Layered Architectures Are So Darn Cool

Layered architectures let us cheat complexity. Instead of making a single über-complicated brain, we build simple brains stacked on top of each other that specialize in what they're good at.
It's like building a superhero team:

One handles emergencies.

One handles planning.

One handles resource management.

Put them together, and boom—you get an agent that's ready to handle real life's chaos (and maybe even a rogue cat or two).

Conclusion: Stack It Till You Make It

Layered architectures are like building a cognitive sandwich—every layer has a role, and when you put them together, you get something greater than the sum of its parts. They allow AI agents to think fast when needed, plan deeply when time allows, and adapt on the fly when reality inevitably throws a wrench into the works.

Sure, sometimes the layers argue like a dysfunctional family at Thanksgiving, but with good design, they can pull off some seriously impressive feats.

(And remember: life's all about layers—whether you're building AI or eating cake. Choose wisely.)

5.4 Subsumption and Behavior-Based Design

Alright, quick story: when I first started working with robots way back in the day, I thought making them "think" like little philosophers would be the peak of genius. Turns out, when your bot is on fire because it couldn't plan fast enough to not crash into a wall, you learn a hard truth: sometimes thinking too much is dangerous.

This epiphany led Rodney Brooks, one of the legends of AI and robotics, to say, "Hey, what if we just... did stuff instead of wasting time thinking about it first?" Thus was born subsumption architecture—the wild, rebellious cousin of deliberative systems—and behavior-based design followed not far behind.

What is Subsumption Architecture?

Subsumption architecture is a layered, behavior-driven approach where lower layers control immediate, simple behaviors, and higher layers can override or "subsume" those behaviors when needed.

In other words:

Low-level layers: Handle urgent, basic needs (e.g., don't crash into walls).

Mid-level layers: Take care of slightly more complex behaviors (e.g., follow a path).

High-level layers: Pursue strategic goals (e.g., explore the map).

But—and this is key—each layer is built independently and can override the behavior of the layers beneath it if necessary.

Imagine a robot with:

A bottom layer to avoid obstacles,

A middle layer to wander around exploring,

A top layer trying to reach a specific destination.

If the top layer sees an open path, it tells the robot to move forward. But if suddenly a kitten leaps into the way, the bottom "avoid obstacle" layer immediately kicks in to steer clear, without waiting for the top layer to analyze kitten physics. Smart, right?

Core Principles of Behavior-Based Design

Behavior-based design follows a few key mantras:

Action over Deliberation

Agents should act quickly based on current perceptions, not sit around constructing detailed world models.

Parallel, Decentralized Control

Different behaviors operate simultaneously and independently. No single "master plan" bottlenecks the system.

Emergence over Explicit Programming

Complex behavior emerges from the interaction of simple behaviors, rather than being explicitly hardcoded.

It's not about controlling everything perfectly—it's about letting good enough behaviors swarm together into useful, adaptable intelligence.

How It Works in Practice

Let's take an example: a robot vacuum cleaner (yep, the noble Roomba).

Low layer: Detects walls and furniture and avoids them.

Middle layer: Seeks dirty spots and moves toward them.

Top layer: Maps rooms over time and prioritizes high-traffic areas.

The vacuum doesn't sit down and "think" about how dirty your living room is. It reacts, navigates, and learns dynamically based on layers working independently and efficiently.

If the bottom layer senses a table leg, the vacuum doesn't politely ask the top layer for permission—it immediately adjusts course. Quick, simple, effective.

Advantages of Subsumption and Behavior-Based Systems

Why has this design stuck around for decades? Let's break it down:

Speed and Reactivity

No complex planning delays mean the agent can respond almost instantly to changes.

Robustness

If one behavior fails, others still operate. No single point of catastrophic failure.

Scalability

New behaviors can be added by stacking new layers on top, without rewiring everything.

Simplicity of Design

Each layer can be designed and tested separately. Much easier than one gigantic brain model.

Limitations of Subsumption and Behavior-Based Systems

Of course, this "act fast, think later" model isn't perfect:

Limited Long-Term Planning

These systems can struggle with tasks requiring detailed foresight or complex sequences of actions.

Behavior Conflicts

If layers aren't carefully prioritized, the robot might act confused—tugged between different behaviors.

No Internal World Model

Without a model of the environment, agents might repeat mistakes or fail to optimize their behavior over time.

Real-World Applications

Subsumption and behavior-based designs are everywhere, especially in scenarios where reactivity matters most:

Mobile Robotics

Mars rovers, autonomous drones, and rescue bots often use layered, behavior-based control to survive hostile environments.

Entertainment Robots

Remember Sony's AIBO robotic dog? Classic example: layers of playful, reactive behaviors stitched together.

Swarm Robotics

Groups of tiny robots that act individually based on simple rules but collectively create complex behaviors (like ants).

Game AI

Many non-player characters (NPCs) in games use behavior-based systems to act unpredictably but believably.

Why It's Still Awesome Today

In an age where AI headlines are dominated by deep learning and multi-billion-parameter models, behavior-based design remains relevant because it reminds us of something crucial:

Sometimes intelligence isn't about thinking harder. It's about reacting smarter.

Even the flashiest AI struggles with real-world chaos, where sensors are noisy, batteries die, and kids throw soccer balls at your robots. Behavior-based agents embrace the chaos and dance with it.

Conclusion: Embrace the Mayhem, One Layer at a Time

Subsumption and behavior-based design teach us that action often trumps overthinking, especially when reality refuses to sit still. It's like life: no amount of planning will ever fully prepare you for the moment your cat decides your Roomba is a mortal enemy.

Building agents that layer smart reactions into emergent behavior gives them a fighting chance to survive, thrive, and maybe even impress us humans with their scrappy, clever antics.

(And if you ever doubt the power of simple behaviors stacked together, just watch a toddler outwit a team of adults at hide-and-seek. Pure, beautiful chaos—just like a well-built AI agent.)

5.5 Selecting the Right Architecture for a Task

Picture this: you're building an AI agent. You've given it sensors, actuators, and a shiny new brain... but now you face the real boss battle: choosing the right architecture. It's a little like choosing the right vehicle for a cross-country trip. You wouldn't drive a go-kart across the desert (well, not unless you enjoy suffering). Similarly, you wouldn't use a complex deliberative architecture for a fast-paced, real-time drone swarm.
Fit matters. Big time.

Choosing an AI architecture isn't about which one sounds cooler or uses fancier jargon. It's about matching what your agent needs to do with how it's going to do it—balancing speed, complexity, environment, goals, and resources like the finely-tuned mad scientist you are.

Factors to Consider When Choosing Architecture

Let's dig into the major elements you need to juggle before crowning an architecture king (or queen):

1. Task Complexity

Simple tasks (like avoiding obstacles) are great for reactive architectures.

Complex tasks (like long-term mission planning) demand deliberative or hybrid architectures that can think several moves ahead.

If your agent's to-do list looks like "stay alive and don't crash," keep it simple. If it's "colonize Mars and survive harsh conditions for ten years," better load up on cognitive horsepower.

2. Environment Predictability

Stable, predictable environments (like factory floors) work fine with simple, reactive agents.

Unpredictable, dynamic environments (like city streets) need architectures capable of planning, adapting, and learning.

If the world your agent lives in changes faster than a toddler's snack preferences, you're going to need some serious adaptability.

3. Speed and Responsiveness Requirements

High-speed tasks need reactive or subsumption-based systems that don't stop to think.

Slow, strategic tasks allow room for more deliberation and layered thinking.

If milliseconds matter (like in drone racing), you can't afford the luxury of deep philosophical pondering.

4. Available Computational Resources

Limited processing power? Go for lightweight, behavior-based designs.

Ample computational muscle? Then hybrid systems blending planning, learning, and reactivity are fair game.

Remember: your AI can't think deep thoughts if its "brain" is basically a potato running on a car battery.

5. Need for Learning and Adaptation

Static agents (doing the same job forever) can use rule-based systems.

Agents that need to adapt over time require learning agents with memory, feedback loops, and evolving strategies.

Basically: is your agent a one-hit wonder or a lifelong learner?

Common Architectures and Their Best Fit

Let's go speed dating with the major architecture types:

Architecture	Best For	Weakness
Reactive	Fast responses, real-time actions	Dumb as a rock at long-term planning
Deliberative	Complex planning, goal achievement	Slow, sometimes fatally so
Layered	Balanced complexity, multitasking	Coordination overhead
Subsumption	Survival in unpredictable environments	Lacks deep strategy
Hybrid	Complex, dynamic tasks needing adaptability	Harder to build, more resource-heavy

Each has its own superpower—and kryptonite. Pick wisely.

Real-World Examples

To make this less theoretical and more "Aha!", let's throw down some real-world case studies:

Warehouse Robots

→ Reactive + Layered. Dodge shelves, deliver packages fast.

Autonomous Cars

→ Hybrid Systems. Must react instantly and plan routes safely.

Space Exploration Rovers

→ Deliberative + Reactive backup. Plan far ahead but survive sudden sandstorms.

Smart Home Assistants

→ Layered Architectures. Answer immediately ("What's the weather?") while managing longer-term tasks ("Schedule a meeting next week.").

Your mission, should you choose to accept it: match the architecture to the mission profile, not your personal preference for what's "cool."

A Step-by-Step Selection Strategy

Here's a cheat sheet for architecture matchmaking:

Define the task clearly.

What exactly does the agent need to do?

Analyze the environment.

Is it static or dynamic? Friendly or hostile?

Set speed and responsiveness priorities.

Real-time or can afford planning time?

Evaluate resources.

How much computational power and memory is available?

Assess the need for adaptability.

Will your agent face evolving challenges?

Prototype quickly.

Test a small-scale version. Agents will often tell you what they hate.

Iterate ruthlessly.

No architecture is perfect out of the box. Adjust, blend, refine.

Remember: it's better to start with something functional than to chase perfection and never launch.

Conclusion: Architecture is Destiny

In AI agent design, choosing the right architecture is like setting the DNA. It will shape everything your agent can—and can't—do.

Pick wrong, and you'll be duct-taping fixes onto a system that was never meant for its world. Pick right, and you'll have an agent that thrives, survives, and maybe even outsmarts a few humans along the way.

(And hey, if you ever pick wrong, don't worry too much. In AI engineering, as in life, a lot of breakthroughs happen when something gloriously breaks. So buckle up, build boldly, and always—always—bring an extra layer of duct tape.)

Chapter 6: Environment Modeling

An agent without an understanding of its environment is like a raccoon with a map of the moon—lost, confused, and possibly up to no good. In this chapter, we train agents to make sense of their surroundings, even if those surroundings are chaotic, unpredictable, or entirely imaginary. Spoiler: the world is never as simple as we hope.

This chapter explores how AI agents perceive and model their environments to make informed decisions. We classify environments by characteristics such as observability, determinism, and dynamism. Topics include internal environment representation, sensor data acquisition, belief state updates, and strategies for real-time adaptation to changing environments.

6.1 Types of Environments (Fully vs. Partially Observable, Deterministic vs. Stochastic, etc.)

Welcome to the wild world of AI environments, where your poor little agent has to survive whatever madness you, nature, or a bunch of mischievous engineers throw at it.
One of the first things you need to wrap your brain around when designing or deploying an agent is what kind of environment it's going to live in. Because, let's be honest— dropping a carefully crafted deliberative robot into a chaotic, unpredictable environment without proper preparation is like sending a porcelain doll into a demolition derby. Spoiler alert: it's not going to end well.

So, let's break down the main flavors of environments and what they mean for our brave AI agents.

Fully Observable vs. Partially Observable

Fully Observable

- A fully observable environment is one where the agent's sensors have access to the complete state of the environment at any given time.
- No secrets. No mysteries. No "what just happened?" moments.

Example:

Chess: Every piece, every move is visible to both players.

A factory assembly line monitored by high-precision sensors.

Why it matters:

In fully observable environments, agents can make decisions based on complete information. Planning becomes more straightforward, and uncertainty is minimized. Agents can behave like mini know-it-alls... and for once, that's a good thing.

Partially Observable

In a partially observable environment, the agent's sensors cannot access the full state. Information may be missing, noisy, or downright deceptive.

Example:

Driving a car in heavy fog.

Navigating a conversation when you can't tell if someone's joking or not.

Why it matters:

Here, the agent needs memory, belief states, and often probabilistic reasoning. It's like navigating with a blindfold and occasionally peeking—your agent needs to infer what's happening beyond its direct perception.

Pro Tip:

If the environment is only partially observable, make sure your agent isn't an impulsive fool. It'll need strategies for dealing with uncertainty, like belief updating and prediction models.

Deterministic vs. Stochastic

Deterministic

In deterministic environments, the next state is completely determined by the current state and the agent's action.

No dice rolls. No random acts of chaos.

Example:

Solving a Rubik's Cube.

Programming a robotic arm on a production line.

Why it matters:

In deterministic settings, agents can plan deep, perfect sequences without worrying about randomness crashing the party. Planning algorithms like A* search thrive here.

Stochastic

In stochastic environments, the outcome of an action is unpredictable, even if the current state and action are known.

Example:

Rolling dice in a board game.

Driving in unpredictable traffic conditions (because you never know when someone will do something truly bananas).

Why it matters:

Here, agents must be designed with probabilities and risk management in mind. No matter how well the agent plans, chance can—and will—intervene.

Survival Tip:

Agents working in stochastic environments should focus on strategies that handle risk gracefully rather than assuming perfect outcomes. Think "Plan A... and a Plan B, C, D, and E just in case."

Episodic vs. Sequential

Episodic

In episodic environments, the agent's experience is divided into atomic "episodes," and what happens in one episode doesn't affect the next.

Example:

Sorting mail into bins.

Playing a hand of poker (each hand is independent, unless you're a world-class hustler).

Why it matters:

These environments simplify decision-making because agents don't have to remember the past. Each decision is made in isolation.

Sequential

In sequential environments, current decisions impact future states.

Example:

Planning a vacation itinerary.

Training a dog not to eat your couch.

Why it matters:

Here, agents need long-term planning and foresight. It's not just about immediate gratification; it's about thinking several moves ahead.

Static vs. Dynamic

Static

- In static environments, the world stays put while the agent thinks.
- It's like the universe pauses politely while your agent scratches its head.

Example:

Filling out a tax form online (well, assuming the internet doesn't crash mid-form).

Why it matters:

Planning and computation are much easier when the world doesn't change while you deliberate.

Dynamic

Dynamic environments change independently of the agent—sometimes aggressively so.

Example:

Piloting a drone through a thunderstorm.

Playing multiplayer video games.

Why it matters:

Agents here need real-time decision-making and situational awareness. If they stand still thinking too long, they get steamrolled.

Discrete vs. Continuous

Discrete

Discrete environments have a finite number of states, actions, and perceptions.

Example:

Tic-Tac-Toe.

Inventory management systems.

Why it matters:

Easier to model, simulate, and solve. Great for training agents with limited brains and plenty of computational handholding.

Continuous

Continuous environments have infinitely many states and actions, often involving real numbers.

Example:

Autonomous car navigation (position, speed, steering angles, oh my).

Flight control systems.

Why it matters:

These require advanced mathematical tools like calculus and differential equations. Planning and control are far trickier here.

Real-World Environment Mashups

Of course, many real-world environments are a messy cocktail of all the above:

Partially observable? Check.

Stochastic? Double check.

Sequential, dynamic, and continuous? Oh boy, triple check.

Think about self-driving cars: they face moving obstacles, unpredictable human behavior, incomplete data from sensors, and continuous control decisions. Designing agents for real-world use isn't about checking a single box; it's about handling the messy overlap of every environmental challenge imaginable.

Conclusion: Know Your Battlefield

At the end of the day, your agent's intelligence doesn't exist in a vacuum. It's tested, stretched, and sometimes humbled by the environment it lives in.

Before building your agent, diagnose the environment like a field medic. Is it friendly or hostile? Predictable or chaotic? Clear or murky? Every answer shapes what kind of architecture, decision-making, and strategies your agent will need to survive—and thrive.

(And if all else fails, remember: even the best AI agent can only do so much. Sometimes, when the raccoon breaks loose at the party, you just gotta grab a broom and roll with it.)

6.2 Representing the Environment Internally

Okay, so your AI agent is out there in the wild, trying to make sense of a world that's messy, noisy, and not exactly designed for its convenience. It's kind of like dropping a kid into a shopping mall with no map and telling them to find the candy store, only the candy store keeps moving and sometimes turns into a shoe shop when you blink.

How does an agent make any smart decisions in such madness?

By building an internal representation of the environment.

This "mental map" is what lets the agent survive, adapt, and maybe even thrive. Without it, even the most sophisticated AI would be like a headless chicken in a windstorm.

Let's dig into how agents create, use, and update these internal models—and how you, brilliant architect of synthetic life, can help them not walk straight into a wall.

Why Build an Internal Representation?

Imagine trying to drive a car with your eyes closed, guessing where the road is based only on engine sounds. That's what it's like for an agent without a proper internal model. The world is big, complicated, and way too much to fully sense in real-time.
Thus, agents build simplified models that capture:

What parts of the world matter

What's likely to happen next

What goals are achievable

An internal representation acts like a shortcut to understanding, compressing massive chaos into manageable information.

Pro Tip:

Better models = better predictions = better decisions.

Garbage models = garbage results. ("Garbage in, garbage out," as every engineer has muttered under their breath at some point.)

Types of Internal Representations

Depending on how fancy (and how memory-hungry) your agent is, there are a few major types of internal models it might build:

1. State-Based Representations

In state-based systems, the agent keeps track of the current state of the environment and uses it to predict outcomes.

Example:

A chess-playing agent maintains the full board position at all times.

Strengths:

Great for fully observable, deterministic environments.

Weaknesses:

Falls apart in dynamic, partially observable worlds unless heavily supplemented.

2. Feature-Based Representations

Rather than modeling the whole environment, the agent extracts and focuses on key features that matter.

Example:

A self-driving car tracks nearby vehicle positions, traffic lights, and lane markings but ignores irrelevant graffiti on walls.

Strengths:

Efficient, scalable to large environments.

Weaknesses:

Risk of missing crucial information if feature selection is poor.

3. Probabilistic Models

When certainty is out the window (hello, real life), agents can use probabilistic models to maintain beliefs about the world.

Example:

A delivery robot might have a 70% belief that a hallway is clear and a 30% belief that it's blocked by a cart.

Strengths:

Handles uncertainty gracefully.

Weaknesses:

More computationally demanding.

4. Relational and Graph-Based Representations

For environments rich in relationships (not the emotional kind—no dating apps for robots... yet), agents can use graphs to represent entities and their connections.

Example:

Social network analysis.

Map-based navigation using nodes and edges.

Strengths:

Excellent for structured, interconnected environments.

Weaknesses:

Managing and updating graphs can get messy.

Building and Updating Internal Models

Agents don't just build a model once and call it a day.

Nope—they need to constantly update their internal worldviews because things change, often when you least expect it.

The key steps are:

Sensing:

Gather raw data through sensors.

Perception:

Process and filter that data into meaningful information.

Belief Update:

Adjust the internal model based on new information.

Prediction:

Use the updated model to guess what might happen next.

Decision:

Choose actions based on the model and predicted outcomes.

This loop happens over and over, often hundreds or thousands of times per second in real-world applications. (Meanwhile, I still sometimes forget why I walked into a room.)

Trade-offs in Representation

Of course, not everything is sunshine and unicorns.

Choosing the right internal model involves serious trade-offs:

Complexity vs. Speed:

Detailed models are accurate but slow. Simplified models are fast but may miss important info.

Memory Use vs. Generalization:

Rich models eat memory like a stoner at a pizza buffet. Sparse models are easier to manage but may struggle with edge cases.

Accuracy vs. Robustness:

Super-specific models may be brittle. Looser models may be more forgiving when the unexpected happens.

Real-World Example: Roomba's Mental Map

- Ever watched a Roomba bump around a room like it's either drunk or on a personal quest for enlightenment?
- Early models were purely reactive—no internal maps.

Later models began mapping room layouts, learning where walls, furniture, and "danger zones" (like staircases) are.

The difference is massive:

Early Roombas: Random wandering, frequent repetition, less efficient cleaning.

Modern Roombas: Systematic cleaning paths, optimized coverage, way fewer existential crises.

Moral of the story:

Even a vacuum cleaner can get a huge upgrade in intelligence just by building a decent mental model of its world.

Conclusion: Mental Models Are the Unsung Heroes

Without an internal representation, even the smartest agent is just a goldfish flailing in a hurricane.

Models give agents the superpower of foresight, letting them act smartly in a world that is often messy, noisy, and unfair.

Choosing the right kind of internal representation—and updating it wisely—is absolutely critical for building AI agents that don't just survive but dominate in their environments.

(And hey, if all else fails, you can always teach your agent to fake it till it makes it. Humans have been getting away with that strategy for millennia.)

6.3 Sensors and Data Acquisition

Alright, let's be honest.

No matter how intelligent or high-tech an agent is, without sensors, it's like a brilliant mind trapped in a sensory deprivation tank. Impressive brainpower, sure—but absolutely no clue whether it's raining outside or if the neighbor's cat just triggered World War III.

Sensors and data acquisition are the agent's lifeline to reality.

This is how agents see, hear, feel, and taste (okay, maybe not taste—unless you're building a robotic food critic, in which case, call me).

Today, we dive into how sensors feed crucial data to our agents, how they grab this information from a chaotic world, and how the whole thing sometimes goes hilariously wrong (and how we fix it).

The Role of Sensors in AI Agents

Imagine sending a secret agent into a spy mission... blindfolded, ear-plugged, and wearing oven mitts.
Not a great strategy.

Similarly, AI agents rely on sensors to:

Detect changes in the environment

Gather information about objects, obstacles, and goals

Monitor internal conditions (like battery level for a robot)

Without sensors, agents would just sit around making wild guesses.

(Which, frankly, sounds like how I wrote my first research paper in college.)

Types of Sensors in AI Systems

There's a sensor for nearly every sense you can imagine—and even a few you can't.

1. Vision Sensors

Cameras: From basic webcams to high-res stereoscopic rigs.

Lidar: Light Detection and Ranging, creating 3D maps with laser beams.

Infrared Sensors: For night vision or heat detection.

Example:

Self-driving cars use lidar to create real-time 3D maps of their surroundings, spotting other vehicles, pedestrians, and the occasional rogue shopping cart.

2. Auditory Sensors

Microphones: For capturing sound.

Ultrasonic Sensors: For measuring distance via sound waves.

Example:

Virtual assistants like Alexa use microphones to pick up your voice (and your tragic attempt to sing along to 90's pop).

3. Touch and Force Sensors

Pressure Sensors: Detecting force or strain.

Tactile Sensors: Simulating the human sense of touch.

Example:

Robotic arms equipped with tactile sensors can adjust their grip so they don't crush a delicate wine glass (or a fragile human ego).

4. Proprioceptive Sensors

Gyroscopes, Accelerometers: For balance, orientation, and motion detection.

Example:

Drones use gyros and accelerometers to stay level mid-flight, even when a gust of wind decides to play dirty.

5. Environmental Sensors

Temperature Sensors: Hot or cold, friend?

Humidity Sensors: How sweaty is the room?

Gas Sensors: Is there a gas leak?

Example:

Smart thermostats use temperature and humidity sensors to keep you comfortable—and to quietly judge your indecision about setting the thermostat.

The Data Acquisition Process

Now that we know agents have all these snazzy sensors, the real fun begins: actually getting and using the data.

Here's the basic flow:

1. Sensing

Sensors collect raw signals from the environment—light, sound, pressure, whatever's relevant.

2. Signal Conditioning

These raw signals often need cleaning. You wouldn't serve unfiltered coffee to a guest (unless you hate them), and you shouldn't serve raw signals to your AI.

Filtering out noise

Amplifying weak signals

Converting signals into a usable format

3. Analog-to-Digital Conversion (ADC)

Most sensors spit out analog data, but agents speak digital. ADC transforms wavy analog signals into lovely, tidy 1s and 0s.

4. Data Processing and Fusion

Often, data from multiple sensors gets merged into one coherent story—a technique called sensor fusion.

Example:

A self-driving car might combine camera vision, radar, and GPS data to understand not just where it is, but where everything else is too.

Challenges in Sensing and Data Acquisition

If this all sounds neat and tidy, allow me to stomp all over that illusion with my muddy boots.

Real-world sensing is messy.

Common problems include:

Noise: Random variations that corrupt the signal.

Latency: Delays between sensing and data processing.

Inaccuracy: Sensors can drift over time or get miscalibrated.

Partial Observability: Sometimes the agent can only see part of the environment.

Sometimes a sensor tells you the object is three feet away when it's actually three inches—and that's how you get hilarious videos of delivery robots ramming into walls.

Fun Fact:

Some agents are designed with redundant sensors—kind of like having two alarm clocks set at once—to make sure that even if one lies to you, the other can snitch.

Strategies for Better Sensing

To deal with all the chaos, good engineers (like your future self) implement smart strategies:

Calibration: Regularly adjusting sensors to maintain accuracy.

Filtering Algorithms: Such as the famous Kalman filter, which smooths out noisy data.

Sensor Fusion: Combining multiple data sources to fill in the gaps.

Error Detection: Algorithms that recognize when sensor readings are suspiciously fishy.

Bottom line:

Good data in = good decisions out. Garbage data in = expensive robots doing dumb things.

Real-World Example: Mars Rovers

NASA's Mars rovers like Curiosity and Perseverance are basically the gods of sensor usage:

Cameras for vision

Spectrometers for chemical analysis

Thermometers for environmental conditions

Ground-penetrating radar

All running hundreds of millions of miles away, with no tech support except some very stressed engineers on Earth.

The rovers' survival depends entirely on smart sensor use and meticulous data acquisition.

(And a little bit of pure, stubborn luck.)

Conclusion: Sensing is Believing (Sort Of)

In the grand adventure of AI agents, sensors are the eyes, ears, and feelers that connect mind to world.

Without them, agents are just code floating in a vacuum.

Mastering sensors and data acquisition means creating agents that aren't just smart in theory—they're smart where it matters most: in messy, unpredictable reality.

(And if your agent ever gets confused despite all your hard work, just remember: even humans sometimes walk into glass doors.)

6.4 Updating the Agent's Belief State

Picture this:

You're driving to work, convinced you know the route like the back of your hand. But midway, you hit unexpected road construction. Suddenly, that mental map you were using? Outdated. You have to quickly update your beliefs about the road layout—or spend the morning trapped in a tragic loop of wrong turns and existential dread.

AI agents face the same problem.

They must continuously update their belief state—their internal understanding of the world—based on new observations, evidence, and experiences. Without this crucial step, an agent would be stuck making decisions based on old, inaccurate information. Not ideal when dodging obstacles, chasing goals, or trying to avoid stepping on virtual Lego bricks.

What Is a Belief State?

Let's get fancy for a second.

An agent's belief state is its internal representation of what it thinks the environment looks like. Not necessarily what it actually is—because, much like humans, agents operate with incomplete, noisy, or outdated information.

In a perfect world:

The agent's belief state = the real world exactly.

In the real world:

The agent's belief state = a reasonable guess.

This internal model helps the agent predict outcomes, plan actions, and avoid blunders like thinking a shadow is an object (happens to the best of us).

Why Updating Matters

Imagine an agent that's navigating a dynamic environment, like a robot vacuum in a messy living room.

If someone suddenly drops a pile of laundry on the floor, the robot's original belief ("The floor is clear!") is now dangerously false. If it doesn't update its belief state, it might:

Plow into the laundry at full speed.

Waste time recalculating routes based on wrong assumptions.

Get stuck in a feedback loop of failure and sadness.

Updating the belief state = giving your agent fresh glasses for a clear view of reality. Without updates, even the smartest agent would be flying blind.

How Belief States Are Updated

So how does an agent go from "I think the world looks like this" to "Whoa, update: new obstacles detected"?

The process generally follows these steps:

1. Perceive

Sensors collect new data from the environment (refer back to our earlier chapter on sensors and data acquisition).

2. Interpret

The agent processes this sensor data to identify changes or new information.

3. Merge

The new information gets integrated into the existing belief state.

4. Revise

Conflicting or outdated beliefs are adjusted or discarded to maintain an accurate and useful model.

Pro Tip:

Good agents don't overreact to a single weird piece of sensor data. Instead, they use probabilistic models to weigh how likely a change really is before tossing out old beliefs.

Methods for Belief Updating

There are several tried-and-true methods agents use, depending on how sophisticated (and paranoid) they are.

1. Simple Overwrite

The agent simply trusts new observations and updates its belief accordingly.

Example:

If the camera sees an obstacle at (x, y), the agent updates its map with "Obstacle present at (x, y)."

Downside: If the sensor glitched, the agent might mistakenly believe there's a ghost wall. Spooky.

2. Probabilistic Updating

Instead of flipping its belief with every new piece of data, the agent adjusts its confidence levels.

Example:

The agent thinks there's an 80% chance an object is in a location based on multiple noisy observations.

This is especially useful in partially observable environments where one faulty reading could otherwise cause chaos.

3. Bayesian Updating

For the nerds (and I say that lovingly because I'm one), Bayesian inference provides a mathematically rigorous way to update beliefs.

Formula in spirit:

New belief = (Old belief × Likelihood of evidence) / Normalizing constant

Translation:

If the evidence supports the belief, boost your confidence. If it contradicts it, lower your confidence. Easy math, right? (Just kidding, it can make your brain hurt.)

Belief State Representations

Depending on the complexity of the agent and the environment, belief states can be represented in several ways:

State Vectors: For simple environments with finite states.

Probability Distributions: For uncertain or noisy environments.

Logical Sentences: For agents working in more abstract spaces (like theorem provers or dialogue systems).

Occupancy Grids: Common for robotic mapping (dividing space into a grid where each cell is marked occupied, free, or unknown).

Each representation has its pros and cons. Choose wisely, young Padawan.

Real-World Examples

Self-Driving Cars:

Update belief states continuously with lidar, cameras, GPS, and radar. If a construction zone appears or a pedestrian jaywalks, the car's belief about the environment must instantly adapt.

Video Game AI:

Enemies update their belief states about the player's position based on sound or sight cues. If they hear a noise but don't see you, they might suspect your presence without knowing exactly where you are. (Just like a cat who knows you touched its tail but can't prove it.)

Delivery Robots:

Regularly update maps to account for moving obstacles like crowds, furniture rearrangements, or that one guy who refuses to walk in a straight line.

Challenges in Belief Updating

Nothing's ever easy, right? Common challenges include:

Noisy Data: Garbage in, garbage out.

Computational Complexity: Constantly updating a complex belief state is resource-intensive.

Partial Observability: Sometimes the agent can't see everything it needs to.

Latency: Delays in processing can cause the belief state to be "out of date" even before the update is complete.

Smart agents need clever algorithms to overcome these issues—balancing accuracy, speed, and resource usage like pros.

Conclusion: Trust, But Verify

Updating an agent's belief state is not just a nice-to-have; it's survival for intelligent behavior.

It's what separates smart, adaptable agents from clueless bots that bump into walls and embarrass themselves (and, let's be honest, their creators too).

A well-updated belief state means better decisions, quicker adaptations, and smoother performance—even when the world throws a wrench, a cat, or a rogue laundry pile into the mix.

(And remember: if your agent ever stubbornly refuses to update its belief state despite overwhelming evidence, congratulations—you've just built a teenager.)

6.5 Real-Time Adaptation to Environment Changes

You know those action movies where the hero has to improvise because absolutely everything goes wrong? Yeah, welcome to real-time adaptation for AI agents.
Imagine sending a robot to deliver coffee across a bustling office floor. Ten seconds in, its path is blocked by a rogue chair, two distracted humans, and somebody's emotional support iguana. If it can't adapt right now, your poor robot might end up wearing the coffee instead of delivering it.

Real-time adaptation is about AI agents reacting instantly—or at least fast enough—to sudden, unpredictable changes in their environment. It's like mental parkour: sensing, deciding, and acting all in the blink of an eye.

Why Real-Time Adaptation Matters

Let's be real—the real world is messy.

Environments rarely sit still, especially when humans, animals, weather, or technology are involved. An AI agent can plan all it wants, but if it can't pivot on a dime when things change, it's going to crash, freeze, or make hilariously bad decisions.

Without real-time adaptation, an agent becomes obsolete faster than a GPS that still thinks roads built in 2006 are "future projects."

Agents need to:

Detect changes (new obstacles, missing objects, moving targets)

Assess impact (is this change critical?)

Replan or adjust (find a new path, modify goals, recalibrate actions)

Do it fast enough to stay effective

Otherwise, your "smart" drone becomes a very expensive lawn dart.

Core Ingredients for Real-Time Adaptation

Building a real-time adaptive agent isn't just bolting a panic button onto a basic system. It requires deep integration of several powerful capabilities:

1. Fast Perception

The agent needs sensors that can pick up changes immediately.

Cameras, lidar, sonar, accelerometers—whatever gives fresh, accurate readings with minimal lag.

2. Continuous Belief Updating

We just talked about belief states.

Real-time agents must constantly update their beliefs—not every minute, but every few milliseconds if possible.

3. Dynamic Planning

Static plans are great... until the world laughs at them.

Real-time agents often use dynamic replanning to adjust their path or action sequence on the fly.

4. Decision-Making Under Uncertainty

It's not enough to recognize a problem.

Agents must decide quickly, sometimes with incomplete data, choosing the action with the best odds of success.

5. Resource Management

All this sensing, thinking, and acting burns computational resources.

A real-time agent must prioritize critical updates and not get bogged down overanalyzing minor details (save that for the post-mission debrief).

Techniques for Real-Time Adaptation

Different environments and agent designs call for different tricks, but here are some crowd favorites:

1. Reactive Planning

Instead of waiting to replan the entire mission, the agent reacts with localized fixes:

Dodge left instead of recalculating a new three-mile path.

Pause when something weird happens, then resume after confirming it's safe.

It's like a shortcut between "Whoa!" and "Got it, moving on."

2. Anytime Algorithms

An agent running an anytime algorithm can return a "good enough" solution almost immediately, then improve it over time if resources allow.

Example:

If a robot needs a new path now, it quickly computes a rough plan to get moving, then refines the route as it goes.

3. Behavior Trees

Popular in game AI and robotics, behavior trees allow agents to quickly switch behaviors based on conditions:

If obstacle ahead → switch to avoidance behavior

If obstacle cleared → resume normal navigation

Behavior trees are simple, modular, and fast—perfect for hectic environments.

4. Reinforcement Learning

Advanced agents can use learned policies to react instantly based on past experiences:

"Last time a red balloon floated by, it meant a kid party was nearby. Best to slow down and proceed carefully."

Learning agents adapt not just to immediate surprises, but to patterns of surprises over time.

Real-World Examples

Self-Driving Cars:

Constantly adapting to reckless drivers, jaywalking pedestrians, sudden weather changes, and the occasional rogue shopping cart.

Warehouse Robots:

Adjusting routes around humans, spilled packages, and mischievous coworkers testing their reflexes with surprise obstacles.

Military Drones:

Replanning missions mid-flight to avoid new threats, changing terrain, or evolving objectives.

Virtual Assistants:

Believe it or not, even chatbots adapt in real-time, adjusting responses based on a user's changing tone, urgency, or context.

Challenges in Real-Time Adaptation

Sure, adapting on the fly sounds heroic, but it's a messy business.

Latency: Sensors and processors aren't infinitely fast. Delays can cause tragicomic missteps.

Noise and False Positives: Not every blip on the radar is a real problem, but treating everything as a five-alarm fire drains resources fast.

Decision Paralysis: In complex environments, too many possibilities can overwhelm the agent if not handled carefully.

Resource Constraints: Real-time processing requires serious computational muscle, which isn't always available (especially in tiny embedded systems).

Building an agent that adapts well in real-time is a constant balancing act between speed, accuracy, and resource usage.

Future Trends: Smarter, Faster, Smoother

Advances in AI hardware, edge computing, and neuromorphic chips are making it easier for agents to react faster and smarter.

Emerging techniques like meta-learning ("learning how to learn") and event-driven computing promise even better real-time adaptation.

Imagine agents that not only react quickly but anticipate changes based on subtle hints—like a seasoned driver slowing down before even seeing the ball roll into the street.

Real-time adaptation will keep evolving, because, frankly, the world isn't getting any simpler.

(And neither are humans, bless our chaotic hearts.)

Conclusion: Stay Agile or Stay Behind

In a world that changes faster than you can say "unexpected server error," real-time adaptation isn't optional—it's survival.

Whether it's a robot, a drone, a virtual assistant, or your future AI butler (still waiting, tech industry), the ability to pivot, replan, and thrive in chaos will separate the winners from the spectacular faceplants.

And hey, if your agent still wipes out sometimes?

No shame. Even the best humans slip on banana peels once in a while. It's what you do next that matters.

Chapter 7: Goal Formulation and Planning

You can't just throw an agent into the world and say, "Be productive!" That's like giving a GPS to someone without telling them where to go. In this chapter, we teach agents to set goals, make plans, and—importantly—not freeze in existential panic when given multiple choices. It's all about smart objectives and even smarter paths.

This chapter provides a comprehensive overview of how agents formulate goals and construct plans to achieve them. It introduces planning algorithms, including search strategies and optimization methods, and explores the use of heuristics to improve efficiency. We also address the challenges agents face when juggling conflicting goals or navigating trade-offs in complex environments.

7.1 Defining Goals and Desires

Let's start with an awkward truth: without goals, AI agents are just... weirdly expensive paperweights.

Imagine building a cutting-edge robot and then forgetting to tell it what it's supposed to do. It would just stand there, blinking, occasionally spinning in place, and possibly questioning its own existence. (Not recommended.)

Defining goals and desires is absolutely critical—it's the difference between a directionless bot and a laser-focused agent that actually gets things done.
In short: goals give an agent purpose. And in AI, purpose is everything.

What Are Goals (and Why Should an AI Care)?

In human terms, a goal is something you want to achieve: get a coffee, run a marathon, finally figure out how to fold a fitted sheet without crying.

In AI terms, a goal is a specific condition or set of conditions that an agent is trying to make true.

Examples:

"Navigate from point A to point B without collisions."

"Sort these packages based on size and weight."

"Answer a user's question accurately and politely."

Desires, on the other hand, are slightly fuzzier. They represent possible goals the agent might want to pursue but hasn't fully committed to yet.

Think of desires as a giant buffet, and goals as the one or two dishes you actually load onto your plate.

In short:

Desires = possibilities

Goals = active missions

And yes, in a complex AI system, an agent might have hundreds of desires but only a handful of actual goals at any given time. (Basically, it's like my New Year's resolutions.)

Formalizing Goals

Okay, jokes aside, how do we technically define goals for AI agents?

Goals are usually represented as logical statements about the environment or the agent's internal state.

For example:

"At(x, y)" → The agent wants to be at coordinates (x, y).

"Delivered(package1, destinationA)" → Package 1 must be delivered to destination A.

In goal-driven systems, these statements are used to:

Formulate plans (How do I get there?)

Evaluate progress (Am I closer to success?)

Decide when to stop (Did I make it?)

This is why formal, precise goal definitions are crucial. If your goal is vague ("Be awesome!"), good luck teaching an agent how to measure or achieve that.

Hard Goals vs. Soft Goals

- Not all goals are created equal.
- In AI, we often distinguish between hard goals and soft goals.

Hard Goals:

- Non-negotiable. The agent must satisfy these, or it has failed.
- (Example: The drone must deliver the package.)

Soft Goals:

- Nice to have, but optional. Meeting them improves performance but isn't mandatory.
- (Example: The drone should also avoid scaring local wildlife while delivering the package.)

In complex systems, balancing hard and soft goals becomes an art form.

Sometimes you'll need to trade off one for the other, and agents must be smart enough to prioritize without melting down.

Goal Generation: Static vs. Dynamic

Some agents operate in environments where their goals are static—set once and never change.

Others live in a glorious, unpredictable world where goals evolve based on:

New information

Environmental changes

Human commands

Internal discoveries (like realizing the initial goal was impossible)

Dynamic goal generation is especially important for:

Game-playing agents (new quests!)

Adaptive robots (unexpected obstacles!)

Virtual assistants (changing user needs!)

It's not just about setting a goal once—it's about constantly revisiting and adjusting goals as the situation demands.

In other words, flexible agents don't just chase carrots; they know when to chase a different carrot, switch to a potato, or just head back to the barn for a nap.

Conflicting Goals and Desires

Sometimes, life (and AI) isn't simple.

Agents often face conflicting goals, like:

Deliver the package quickly vs. Deliver it safely

Maximize profit vs. Minimize risk

Answer user questions accurately vs. Respond quickly

In these cases, agents must:

Prioritize goals (which one matters more?)

Negotiate trade-offs (how much delay is acceptable for safety?)

Use utility functions to mathematically evaluate different outcomes

It's a lot like adulting, honestly. You're constantly juggling competing goals like "save money" and "buy tacos."

Real-World Examples of Goal-Driven Agents

Roombas: Clean the floor. Avoid obstacles. Recharge before dying dramatically in the middle of the living room.

Self-Driving Cars: Transport passengers to their destination safely, legally, and efficiently.

Healthcare Bots: Monitor patient vitals, alert medical staff, and occasionally comfort humans with awkward robot empathy.

Each of these agents has clear goals—without them, they'd just wander aimlessly, possibly scaring children and annoying cats.

Building Goal-Aware Agents: Challenges

Ambiguity: Humans love giving unclear goals ("Make the user happy!") which are murderously difficult to formalize.

Over-Optimization: Agents sometimes achieve the goal... but in horrifyingly literal ways. (Ask any AI researcher about the paperclip maximizer nightmare.)

Dynamic Priorities: Real-time environments often force agents to reprioritize goals on the fly, which requires a lot of brainpower—or at least some cleverly coded shortcuts.

Good goal definition is not just a technical job. It's a weird mix of philosophy, psychology, math, and good old-fashioned common sense.

Conclusion: Goals Are Life (For Agents, Too)

Without goals, an AI agent is just an overengineered lawn ornament.

With goals, it's a purposeful, adaptable, mission-driven entity capable of making decisions, learning from mistakes, and impressing us humans with its uncanny ability to actually get things done.

So, next time you see a smart system navigating a messy world, take a moment to appreciate the quiet power of well-defined goals—and maybe send a silent thank-you to the engineers who spent sleepless nights making sure "Deliver the coffee" didn't somehow turn into "Take over the world."

Because trust me, one misplaced goal could make all the difference.

7.2 Planning Techniques in AI Agents

Imagine this: your agent is a robot trying to get from point A to point B. Simple, right? Just move in a straight line. But what if there's a giant elephant in the way? A sleeping dog? A wall of confetti? Now we need planning. You see, planning in AI is more than just following a path; it's about figuring out how to achieve a goal in a world that loves throwing curveballs. This is where the art of planning comes into play.

In the world of AI agents, planning is the agent's brainchild moment, where it figures out the steps, sequence, and strategy required to achieve its objectives. It's like when you plan your weekend: you start with a vague idea ("I'll relax") but end up with a detailed itinerary involving snacks, Netflix binges, and an elaborate strategy to avoid social obligations. AI agents work similarly, except their weekend is solving real-world problems, and they don't need to worry about bad Wi-Fi or running out of snacks.

What Is Planning in AI?

In simple terms, planning refers to the process of deciding what actions an agent must take to achieve a specific goal. But it's not just about doing things one after another; the magic of planning is in choosing the right actions at the right time. It's about anticipating the future, creating a roadmap, and adjusting when things inevitably go awry.

Planning is critical because agents often work in dynamic environments where conditions change unexpectedly. Consider a robot delivering a pizza: it starts by identifying its route, but suddenly a car pulls up, blocking the sidewalk. The robot has to adapt its plan to navigate around the car. This flexibility is where planning techniques shine.

Types of Planning

There are various planning techniques in AI that can be used depending on the complexity and requirements of the task. Some are more basic, while others allow for deeper decision-making and flexibility.

1. Forward Planning (aka Goal-Stack Planning)

In forward planning, the agent starts at the initial state and works towards the goal step by step. It generates a sequence of actions that take it from the current state to the goal.

This is how you would plan your road trip from point A to point B: first, you choose a route, then make stops, and gradually make progress toward your destination.

Pros: Simple and easy to understand.

Cons: It doesn't always deal well with unexpected changes or obstacles because it doesn't consider the full picture upfront.

2. Backward Planning (aka Goal Regression)

Backward planning is like reverse-engineering a recipe. Instead of starting at the beginning, the agent works backward from the goal state, figuring out which actions will take it there. It asks, "If this is my final destination, what do I need to do right before that? And the step before that?" Think of it like planning your way back to your car in a parking lot after an epic shopping spree—you'll backtrack until you've mapped the whole route.

Pros: Great for problems with a well-defined end goal.

Cons: Not so useful in situations where intermediate steps are unclear or not easily reversible.

3. Hierarchical Planning

If you've ever tried to plan a wedding or organize a conference, you know that you can't just plan everything at once. You need to break it down into smaller, manageable chunks. Hierarchical planning works the same way: it decomposes a larger task into sub-tasks, which are then planned individually before being combined into a larger plan. In the case of the wedding, you might first plan the venue, then the catering, then the guest list, and so on, each step building up to the grand event.

Pros: More flexible and can handle complex problems more effectively.

Cons: Can get very complicated and time-consuming for large-scale tasks.

4. Conditional Planning

In real life, we often make plans that involve contingencies. "If it rains, I'll bring an umbrella; if it doesn't, I'll wear sunglasses." Conditional planning allows agents to create plans that include different courses of action depending on various conditions. For instance, an autonomous vehicle may have a standard route, but it also plans alternate routes in case of traffic, accidents, or road closures.

Pros: Allows agents to react to unexpected changes, making it more adaptable.

Cons: Can become unwieldy if there are too many conditions or branching possibilities.

Planning with Partial Information

In a perfect world, agents would have all the information they need to plan their actions accurately. But the world is messy, and agents rarely have perfect knowledge. Partial information is when an agent doesn't know everything about its environment or situation, but it still needs to plan based on what it knows.

To deal with this, agents use assumptions and probabilistic reasoning. They might assume the layout of a room based on previous experiences, or estimate the chances of traffic based on time of day. This uncertainty is why planning under uncertainty has become a crucial area of AI research.

Planning in Dynamic Environments

We can't ignore the reality that things change, and fast. The robot delivering pizza doesn't know that the sidewalk is going to be blocked by a construction crew until it's already on its way. This is why dynamic planning is necessary: agents must continually reassess and update their plans as they gather more information.

Dynamic planners need to constantly monitor the environment and make adjustments on the fly. A simple reactive plan may not be enough. For example, if the robot detects a new obstacle (like that rogue construction worker), it needs to reevaluate its plan in real-time to find a better path. If it waits too long, the pizza might go cold!

Real-World Applications of Planning in AI

Self-Driving Cars: These cars need to plan their routes, make real-time adjustments based on road conditions, and ensure they obey traffic laws. Their planning systems use a combination of forward and backward planning, layered with real-time updates.

Robots in Manufacturing: These robots need to plan tasks like assembling parts, inspecting goods, or even sorting packages. With dynamic environments and unexpected failures, these robots must be able to plan ahead while adapting to new information.

Game AI: In video games, NPCs (Non-Player Characters) often need to make plans to navigate environments, fight enemies, or react to player actions. The more dynamic the game, the more complex the planning must be.

The Future of Planning in AI

As AI agents become more advanced, planning is getting increasingly sophisticated. Researchers are developing learning-based planners, where agents improve their planning abilities by experiencing more real-world scenarios and adjusting their strategies accordingly. AI planners are also becoming better at working with incomplete or ambiguous information, making them more flexible and efficient.

The future of planning in AI is all about flexibility, speed, and adaptability—ensuring that agents can tackle a wide range of tasks, even when things get unpredictable.

Conclusion: Plan for Success, But Be Ready to Adjust

In the world of AI, planning is both an art and a science. It's about taking what you know, predicting what might happen, and crafting a series of actions that lead to your goal. However, the real genius of AI planning lies in its ability to adapt—because, as we all know, life has a funny way of throwing unexpected challenges your way.

Whether it's robots delivering pizzas or self-driving cars navigating rush hour, the best AI agents are those that can plan smartly and adapt when the unexpected happens. So, next time you see an agent going from point A to point B, remember: it didn't just make a lucky guess. It planned that path like a strategic mastermind—then adjusted it to avoid that elephant in the hallway.

7.3 Search Strategies and Algorithms

AI agents are not mindless wanderers—they need a strategy to find solutions to problems. This is where search strategies and algorithms come into play. Think of an agent as a detective on a case, trying to piece together clues to solve a mystery. The agent has to search through possible clues (or actions, or states), find the most relevant ones, and work towards solving the problem. Without a good search strategy, the agent could end up lost in a maze, just like I do every time I try to navigate IKEA.

When AI agents are given a problem, they need to figure out how to explore all the possible options without getting bogged down in a time-consuming, inefficient search. The faster they find the solution, the better. That's where these search algorithms come in, guiding the agent to the most optimal path.

The Basics of Search in AI

At its core, search refers to the process an AI agent uses to find a solution in a space of possible actions or states. When tasked with a problem, the agent's goal is to identify the best sequence of actions that lead to a goal state, whether that's solving a puzzle, finding a route on a map, or making an optimal decision in a game.

Let's put it into a more relatable example:

Imagine you're at a crossroad and have to choose one of three paths, but you don't know which one leads to your destination. The best you can do is search each path methodically to find the one that gets you there the quickest (or safest, or most efficiently). This is the basic idea of search in AI: exploring the "space" of possibilities and finding the best way forward.

Types of Search Strategies

Now, let's break down the common types of search strategies AI agents use to explore possible solutions.

1. Uninformed Search (Blind Search)

In uninformed search, the agent has no knowledge about the environment or the goal beyond the current state. It blindly explores the search space until it finds the solution. Think of it as the agent just taking random steps forward and hoping for the best.

Some common uninformed search strategies include:

Breadth-First Search (BFS): This strategy explores all possible states at the current depth before moving to the next level. Imagine you're at a party and trying to find the bathroom. BFS would have you check every room on your current floor before going up to the next floor, ensuring you don't miss anything (but also making sure you check every room thoroughly).

Pros: Guaranteed to find the shortest path to the solution.

Cons: Can be inefficient in terms of memory and computation, especially for large spaces.

Depth-First Search (DFS): DFS dives deep into the search space, exploring one path as far as it can go before backtracking and trying another path. It's like choosing a path and following it until you hit a dead-end, then backtracking and trying a new direction.

Pros: More memory-efficient than BFS, as it doesn't need to store as many states.

Cons: It might go down a path that's not the best, taking longer to find the solution.

2. Informed Search (Heuristic Search)

In contrast to uninformed search, informed search uses additional knowledge (a "heuristic") about the environment to guide the search. This heuristic is a function that estimates the cost of reaching the goal from any given state, helping the agent make more informed choices about where to go next.

Common strategies include:

A Search*: This is like BFS with a twist—it uses both the cost to get to a node and an estimate of the remaining cost to reach the goal. The result? A* tends to find the shortest path more efficiently than simple BFS.

Pros: A* is often the most optimal search algorithm for many problems and is quite efficient.

Cons: It requires a good heuristic to work well. If the heuristic is off, A* could perform poorly.

Greedy Search: Greedy search only looks for the next best step, aiming for the goal as quickly as possible based on the current state, without worrying about the bigger picture. It's like heading straight to the snack table at a party without realizing you're avoiding the dance floor.

Pros: Fast and simple.

Cons: It's not always optimal—it might get stuck in a local minimum or miss the overall best path.

Advanced Search Strategies

As AI problems get more complex, simple search strategies often aren't enough. Here are some advanced techniques used to solve larger and more complicated problems.

1. Local Search Algorithms

Local search algorithms are used when the search space is too large to explore exhaustively, and the agent needs to focus on improving its current state. Think of it as playing a game of chess: you might not explore all possible moves at once but instead focus on making the best move from where you are right now.

Hill-Climbing: This algorithm starts from an initial state and keeps moving to neighboring states that are better than the current state, like climbing a hill toward the peak. The idea is to always improve, step by step.

Pros: Simple and effective for many problems.

Cons: Can get stuck in a local maximum and miss the global maximum.

Simulated Annealing: Inspired by the process of heating and then slowly cooling a material to remove imperfections, simulated annealing starts by accepting random moves, even if they seem worse, to avoid getting stuck in local optima. As the search progresses, it becomes more "conservative," accepting only better moves.

Pros: Effective at avoiding local minima.

Cons: It requires fine-tuning the temperature schedule.

2. Genetic Algorithms

These are inspired by natural evolution and work by evolving solutions over time. Agents using genetic algorithms start with a population of possible solutions, evaluate their fitness (how well they solve the problem), and then combine and mutate them to create new solutions.

- **Pros**: Good for complex problems with no clear solution space.
- **Cons**: Can be computationally expensive and slow.

When to Use Which Search Strategy?

Choosing the right search strategy depends on the problem you're solving. If you're solving a straightforward puzzle or game, uninformed search might be enough. For more complex tasks, like navigating a robot or playing a real-time strategy game, informed search or local search may be necessary.

Here's a quick cheat sheet:

Simple, well-defined problems: Use BFS or DFS.

When you need to minimize the cost to the goal: Use A*.

For big, complex problems where the space is too large to explore exhaustively: Use local search or genetic algorithms.

Real-World Applications of Search Algorithms

Navigation Systems: GPS systems use search algorithms like A* to find the fastest route between two points, factoring in real-time traffic conditions.

Robotics: Robots that need to navigate a space, avoid obstacles, and plan their movements use search algorithms to plot their path.

Game AI: From chess to video games, search algorithms help AI decide on moves or actions based on the current game state.

Optimization Problems: Whether it's scheduling tasks or designing a network, search algorithms help find the optimal solution.

Conclusion: Search Is the Foundation of AI

Search is at the core of AI problem-solving. Whether you're navigating a robot through a maze, finding the shortest path on a map, or choosing the best move in a game, search algorithms provide the tools to systematically explore possible solutions. By choosing the right search strategy, you can ensure that your AI agent works efficiently and effectively, avoiding dead ends and finding the best path forward—no blindfolded wandering required.

7.4 Heuristics and Optimization

When it comes to AI problem-solving, optimization is the name of the game. But there's one teeny, tiny problem: solving some problems can be incredibly complex, requiring vast amounts of time and computational power to reach an optimal solution. Enter heuristics—the problem-solving shortcuts that help AI agents find solutions more quickly by making educated guesses about the best way forward. Think of heuristics as the AI version of a "life hack," guiding the agent toward a better solution without needing to check every single possibility.

But here's the catch: just like with life hacks, heuristics don't always guarantee the perfect solution. They're not magic wands, but rather strategies to help make things better in less time. In this subchapter, we'll explore how heuristics help agents optimize their search, how they contribute to faster problem-solving, and where they might stumble (because let's face it, sometimes life hacks go wrong).

What Are Heuristics?

In the context of AI, a heuristic is a rule of thumb, a mental shortcut that an agent uses to make decisions or predictions more efficiently. Heuristics don't promise the perfect solution (that's what we get from optimal algorithms), but they provide a good-enough solution in a fraction of the time.

Take, for example, the A search algorithm* (which we mentioned earlier in the search strategies section). A* is essentially a blend of an informed search algorithm and a heuristic that helps the AI agent estimate the shortest path to the goal. The heuristic function, often called the cost function, evaluates how promising a particular state or action is in getting closer to the goal. If the heuristic is accurate, the agent will find an optimal solution more quickly. If not, it may end up wasting time or missing the best solution.

A simple, real-world example of heuristics is when you're looking for a place to eat. If you want to find a restaurant in a new neighborhood, you might rely on heuristics like, "Restaurants with lots of cars outside are usually good" or "If a place has long lines, it's probably popular and worth checking out." These are not foolproof, but they help you decide where to go without wandering aimlessly around the block for hours.

The Role of Heuristics in AI Optimization

Heuristics are incredibly important in the world of AI, especially when it comes to solving complex problems that involve large search spaces. These are problems where checking every possible outcome is infeasible due to time or resource constraints. By using heuristics, AI agents can eliminate large portions of the search space that are unlikely to lead to good solutions, narrowing down their focus to the most promising possibilities.

In optimization, the goal is to find the best solution or the optimal solution to a problem. However, optimization problems are often very complex and difficult to solve exactly. This is where heuristics play a major role. They allow AI agents to approximate the best solution in a reasonable amount of time, which is often good enough for practical purposes. This is especially important in areas like robotics, autonomous driving, and game AI, where the sheer number of possible outcomes makes exhaustive search methods impractical.

For instance, when an AI agent is planning the path for a robot to move from point A to point B in a large and dynamic environment, using heuristics can help the agent avoid obstacles, calculate the most efficient route, and do all this in real-time without waiting for hours to compute every possible path.

Common Heuristic Techniques

Now that we know heuristics help AI agents speed up the problem-solving process, let's look at a few common techniques used to design heuristics.

1. Greedy Heuristic

The greedy heuristic works by selecting the option that seems the best at each step, with the hope that it leads to the optimal solution. It doesn't consider the big picture; it just looks at the immediate next step. It's a bit like a person trying to climb a hill by always choosing the path that looks the steepest and most direct—hoping it'll lead to the top.

For example, in the A* search algorithm, the greedy heuristic estimates how far a given state is from the goal and always prefers states that bring the agent closer to the goal.

Pros: Greedy algorithms are simple and can be very efficient when used in the right situations.

Cons: They can sometimes lead to poor solutions because they don't consider the full scope of the problem.

2. Admissible Heuristics

An admissible heuristic is one that never overestimates the cost of reaching the goal from any given state. This type of heuristic is key to algorithms like A* because it ensures the algorithm will find the optimal solution. It's like estimating how long a road trip will take—if you know it's at least 5 hours but not more than 8, you're being admissible.

Pros: Guarantees optimal solutions when used with A*.

Cons: May not always be the most efficient.

3. Informed Heuristic

An informed heuristic is a function that gives you some idea of how "good" a state is based on knowledge about the goal. A heuristic that gives better estimates of the remaining cost to reach the goal is considered more informed. This is like using a GPS that factors in live traffic data, roadblocks, and construction when estimating the fastest route. It doesn't just rely on the distance—it knows real-world factors that can affect travel time.

Pros: Greatly speeds up the search and usually leads to better performance.

Cons: Requires a good understanding of the problem and access to relevant data.

Heuristics in Optimization Problems

In optimization problems, heuristics allow AI agents to explore and find solutions in complex spaces where an exhaustive search would be too costly. For example:

Traveling Salesman Problem (TSP): In this problem, the AI needs to find the shortest route that visits several cities and returns to the starting point. Solving it exactly takes an enormous amount of time. But using a heuristic like nearest-neighbor—where the agent always chooses the closest city to visit next—can provide a quick, near-optimal solution.

Job Scheduling: In job scheduling problems, where the goal is to assign tasks to workers in the most efficient way, heuristics like earliest deadline first or longest job first can be used to find a good solution quickly.

Conclusion: Heuristics Make AI Smarter (and Faster)

While heuristics don't guarantee a perfect solution every time, they play a crucial role in enabling AI agents to make quick, intelligent decisions in complex scenarios. Optimization problems are everywhere, from route planning to resource allocation, and heuristics help us find practical solutions without needing to check every single possibility.

So, next time you find yourself solving a problem—whether it's navigating a maze or deciding which pizza to order—remember that a good heuristic can save you time and effort. You don't have to go down every single path to reach your goal. Just take the one that seems the smartest, and if you're lucky, it'll lead you to the optimal solution... or at least a really good pizza.

7.5 Handling Conflicting Goals and Trade-offs

When it comes to AI agents, having multiple goals to pursue is a regular thing. After all, just like humans, agents rarely have a single mission in life. But here's the twist—sometimes these goals are in direct conflict with each other. One goal might require the agent to take one action, while another goal demands an entirely different action. It's like trying to multitask during a dinner party: should you keep chatting with the guests, or focus on not burning the food? This is the reality of conflicting goals in AI systems.

Luckily, AI agents have a few tricks up their sleeves to manage these situations, and trade-offs play a central role in how they navigate these conflicts. In this section, we'll look at how agents prioritize different goals, deal with competing objectives, and use trade-offs to balance multiple demands, all while striving to perform their tasks efficiently. Whether it's deciding between speed and accuracy or choosing between short-term gains and long-term success, AI agents are constantly making tough choices—and that's what makes them smart!

Understanding Conflicting Goals

The challenge of conflicting goals is pretty straightforward: an AI agent is trying to achieve multiple goals, but the goals require mutually exclusive actions. For example, imagine an autonomous vehicle with the goal of reaching a destination as quickly as possible while also maintaining passenger safety. These two goals are in conflict because driving fast could increase the risk of an accident. Thus, the agent has to make decisions that weigh the trade-offs between different objectives.

To handle conflicting goals, AI agents need a system for prioritizing these goals. Depending on the situation, some goals will take precedence over others. The agent will evaluate the importance of each goal and decide which ones are non-negotiable and which ones can be sacrificed to a certain extent. In many cases, agents rely on a form of utility theory or value-based reasoning to assign relative importance to the goals.

For instance, a robot that performs warehouse management might have the goal of completing tasks quickly, but it also has the goal of avoiding collisions with obstacles. If both goals are in conflict, the robot might prioritize avoiding obstacles over speed, as this is crucial to prevent damage to the warehouse and the robot itself. However, if the robot can achieve both goals simultaneously—by adjusting its speed without risking a collision—that's the best scenario.

Trade-offs and Decision Making

Once conflicting goals are identified, AI agents need to make trade-offs between them. This involves balancing the objectives and choosing the best course of action based on the context and constraints. Think of trade-offs as those tough decisions we all face—like choosing between working late to finish a project or going home early to relax. You can't do both, so you make a decision based on what you value more at that moment.

AI agents often use a multi-objective optimization approach to handle these trade-offs. This means they try to optimize multiple conflicting goals at once, often with the help of algorithms that can balance competing objectives. The agent might assign weights to each goal, indicating its relative importance. For example, in the case of the autonomous vehicle, the goal of safety could be weighted more heavily than speed, ensuring that the agent chooses actions that minimize risk.

One well-known method for handling trade-offs is called Pareto optimization. In a Pareto-optimal solution, no objective can be improved without sacrificing another. So, instead of trying to find a perfect solution (which might not exist), the agent looks for a balance where no further improvement can be made without compromising one of the goals. This concept is commonly used in decision-making processes, especially when you have multiple objectives that can't all be fully satisfied at the same time.

Goal Prioritization and Hierarchy

A key aspect of handling conflicting goals is establishing a goal hierarchy. This hierarchy helps agents understand which goals are most critical in certain situations. The agent might have a list of priorities, with some goals ranked higher than others. When faced with a choice between two conflicting goals, the agent can refer to the hierarchy and choose the highest-priority goal, while temporarily disregarding the lower-priority one.

This is especially useful in dynamic environments where the agent's goals may change over time. For instance, in a disaster recovery scenario, an AI agent may initially prioritize saving lives over saving property, but as the situation evolves, the focus might shift to securing resources or managing logistical challenges.

The hierarchy can be predefined or adaptively built through reinforcement learning—where the agent learns from experience and adjusts its priorities based on feedback. This allows the agent to be flexible and responsive in the face of shifting objectives.

Conflict Resolution Strategies

AI agents use several strategies to resolve goal conflicts and minimize the negative impact of trade-offs. Here are a few:

Goal Decomposition

Goal decomposition breaks down complex goals into smaller, more manageable sub-goals. This helps reduce the complexity of decision-making by allowing the agent to focus on individual tasks. For example, in a navigation task, the goal of "get to the destination quickly" can be decomposed into smaller goals like "avoid obstacles" and "optimize speed based on traffic conditions."

Temporal Planning

Sometimes, conflicts arise because goals are time-dependent. The agent might prioritize certain goals at one point in time, but as time passes, it adjusts its goals. For example, a robot cleaning a house might prioritize high-traffic areas at first, then switch to more detailed cleaning tasks once the main areas are finished.

Adaptive Decision-Making

In more advanced AI systems, the agent can adapt its decision-making process based on the environment and the current situation. It might use a machine learning model to predict the future outcomes of different decisions and adjust its priorities accordingly.

Mediating Conflicts

Some agents are designed to mediate between conflicting goals, finding a compromise between them. For example, an AI agent in a smart home might balance energy efficiency with comfort by adjusting the thermostat settings based on current energy costs and the homeowner's preferences.

Conclusion: Embracing the Complexity of Goal Management

Handling conflicting goals and making trade-offs is one of the most fascinating—and challenging—aspects of AI agents. It mirrors the tough decisions we all face in our daily lives, but on a much larger, more complex scale. AI agents need to prioritize their goals, evaluate trade-offs, and make decisions that will lead to the most favorable outcomes. Whether they're driving a car, managing a warehouse, or assisting a user, AI agents are constantly juggling competing objectives, learning from their experiences, and adapting their strategies. So, next time you're balancing competing priorities in your life, just remember—you're in good company with your friendly neighborhood AI agent!

Chapter 8: Learning in AI Agents

There comes a point where agents stop being rule-followers and start asking, "What if I did this differently?" Welcome to the era of learning, where trial, error, and the occasional catastrophe shape intelligence. In this chapter, we unleash agents into the wild and watch as they evolve, adapt, and maybe even outperform their creators.

This chapter focuses on learning paradigms for AI agents, including supervised, unsupervised, and reinforcement learning. It highlights how agents improve through experience, utilize feedback loops, and evaluate performance. We also examine how external knowledge sources can be integrated and discuss continuous learning methods for long-term adaptability.

8.1 Supervised, Unsupervised, and Reinforcement Learning

AI agents aren't born with the knowledge they need to solve problems. No, they're not like your high school self who just instinctively knew how to ace the class presentation. Instead, they learn. Much like how we learn from experience, AI agents can be trained using data, but there are different ways of going about it. This is where supervised learning, unsupervised learning, and reinforcement learning come into play. Think of them as different "learning styles" for AI, each with its own benefits and limitations.

In supervised learning, an agent is given a bunch of labeled examples to learn from—like a teacher giving a student a bunch of flashcards with questions and correct answers on the back. Unsupervised learning, on the other hand, is more like self-study. Here, the AI tries to find patterns in data without anyone handing it the correct answers. Finally, reinforcement learning is like the AI learning through trial and error—think of it as the AI playing a video game and learning from the consequences of its actions, whether it wins or loses.

Supervised Learning: The Teacher's Pet

Let's start with supervised learning, the most traditional approach. In this method, the AI agent learns from a labeled dataset where each input comes with a corresponding correct output (or label). It's kind of like having a teacher guiding the agent through every step of the process.

Imagine you're teaching an AI agent to recognize whether a picture contains a cat or a dog. You show the agent thousands of images, each labeled with either "cat" or "dog." The agent will analyze the features of the images (like shape, color, and texture) and learn to associate these features with the correct label. After enough training, the AI gets pretty good at looking at new images and guessing whether they contain a cat or dog based on what it's learned.

The beauty of supervised learning is that it's easy to understand and implement. The process of labeling data provides clear guidance, making it relatively straightforward to evaluate how well the agent is learning. However, the main downside is that it requires a large amount of labeled data, which can be time-consuming and expensive to produce.

For example, in the real world, supervised learning is used for things like spam email detection (where emails are labeled as "spam" or "not spam") and voice recognition systems (where speech samples are labeled with the correct transcriptions).

Unsupervised Learning: Letting the Agent Figure It Out

Next, let's talk about unsupervised learning, where the AI agent is let loose to explore and learn without any hand-holding. In this method, the agent is given unlabeled data, which means it doesn't have the correct answers to guide it. Instead, the agent's task is to find patterns or structure in the data on its own.

Imagine giving the agent a bunch of photos, but this time, they aren't labeled with anything. The agent has to figure out what the photos have in common. Maybe it groups similar photos together, like finding clusters of pictures with animals, others with landscapes, and so on. This is essentially how clustering works in unsupervised learning. A popular algorithm used for clustering is k-means clustering, where the AI organizes the data into different groups based on similarities.

Another common task in unsupervised learning is dimensionality reduction, where the agent tries to simplify complex data. Imagine you have a dataset with hundreds of features (like measurements of various aspects of flowers), but you don't need all of them to make a good prediction. Principal Component Analysis (PCA) is one method used to reduce the number of features without losing too much information.

Unsupervised learning is incredibly powerful because it doesn't require labeled data, which can be a massive advantage. It's useful for tasks like customer segmentation in marketing, where businesses want to group their customers based on buying behavior, or anomaly detection, which helps in identifying unusual patterns (e.g., fraud detection in banking).

Reinforcement Learning: Learning Through Trial and Error

Now we come to reinforcement learning, which is the closest thing to AI playing a video game and learning from its own mistakes. In this learning method, an agent interacts with an environment and learns by receiving rewards or penalties based on its actions. This is very much like how we learn through trial and error—except the AI agent doesn't get frustrated when it makes mistakes.

Let's break it down: Imagine you're teaching an AI agent to play a game of chess. The agent starts by making random moves, and after each move, it receives feedback: positive feedback (a reward) for making a good move (e.g., capturing an opponent's piece) and negative feedback (a penalty) for making a bad move (e.g., leaving the king in check). Over time, the agent learns which moves lead to more rewards and which lead to penalties, and it adjusts its behavior accordingly.

Reinforcement learning is often used in situations where there's no clear, labeled dataset to learn from. Instead, the agent learns by interacting with its environment and maximizing its reward function. For example, in autonomous driving, the agent learns how to navigate through traffic by receiving rewards for safely reaching its destination and penalties for making dangerous maneuvers.

The core challenge in reinforcement learning is the trade-off between exploration and exploitation. Exploration means trying new actions to discover potentially better strategies, while exploitation means sticking to what you know works. An agent must balance these two to learn efficiently.

The Power of Combining All Three: Hybrid Learning

In many real-world applications, a combination of supervised, unsupervised, and reinforcement learning techniques is used. Hybrid models allow AI agents to take advantage of the strengths of each approach while mitigating their weaknesses. For instance, an agent could be initially trained with supervised learning (to build foundational knowledge), then use unsupervised learning to adapt to new, unlabeled data, and finally use reinforcement learning to fine-tune its behavior based on real-world interactions.

For example, a self-driving car might use supervised learning to recognize objects (like pedestrians and other cars), unsupervised learning to identify new patterns in traffic, and reinforcement learning to improve its driving strategy over time.

Conclusion: The AI Learning Triangle

In the world of AI, supervised, unsupervised, and reinforcement learning each offer a unique approach to training agents. Supervised learning is like having a mentor guide the agent with answers; unsupervised learning lets the agent discover the answers on its own; and reinforcement learning allows the agent to learn by interacting with its environment and adjusting based on feedback. By understanding the strengths and weaknesses of each method, you can choose the best approach for the task at hand—and sometimes, mix and match to get the best of all worlds.

So, next time you hear about an AI agent learning, you can smile knowingly and think, "Ah yes, supervised, unsupervised, or reinforcement learning... every agent has its own style!"

8.2 Adaptability and Experience-Based Learning

In the world of AI, adaptability is one of the key qualities that separates the good from the great. An adaptable agent doesn't just repeat the same task over and over again; it learns from its experiences, figures out what worked (and what didn't), and adjusts its behavior accordingly. This is essentially how human learning works—we get better at things as we experience them. So why should AI be any different? If we want our AI agents to truly be intelligent, they must be able to adapt to new situations, improve over time, and deal with changing environments. Let's dive into experience-based learning and how it empowers agents to handle the unpredictable, the novel, and the downright tricky.

Experience-based learning is all about using past experiences to inform future decisions. Just like how you'd adjust your approach next time you bake cookies based on how the last batch turned out, an AI agent adapts its behavior based on feedback from its environment. This allows it to improve its performance and optimize its actions in future interactions. Think of it as learning by doing, where mistakes are just part of the process and help the agent become better, faster, and smarter. Over time, this experience-based approach allows AI to handle more complex tasks and operate in real-world scenarios that may not be so predictable or well-defined.

The Power of Experience-Based Learning

The beauty of experience-based learning lies in its ability to help AI agents learn from their mistakes—without having to rely on a perfect, pre-defined dataset. It's like when you're learning to ride a bike. At first, you might wobble and fall, but over time, your body learns to balance itself, adjusting to changes in the terrain, your speed, and the obstacles around you. Similarly, an AI agent learns to adapt to new data, new scenarios, and even unpredictable events by using its past experiences to guide its future decisions.

One popular approach to experience-based learning is reinforcement learning (RL), which involves the agent interacting with its environment and receiving feedback based on the actions it takes. These feedback signals (rewards or penalties) are used to adjust the agent's behavior, teaching it to take actions that lead to better outcomes. The more the agent interacts with the environment, the more it refines its strategies and decision-making process.

This learning process is dynamic and iterative, meaning that the agent's actions are constantly improving. Let's take a practical example: an AI agent that plays a video game. In the beginning, the agent might be awful—constantly running into obstacles and losing points. But after playing the game a few times and learning from its mistakes, the agent starts to improve, avoiding obstacles and scoring higher points. It has learned from its past experiences, fine-tuning its behavior to perform better in future rounds. Over time, the agent becomes better than even a human player (yikes!).

Adaptability in Changing Environments

In real-world scenarios, the key to success isn't just about learning from past experiences but also about being able to adapt to new situations. The world isn't static, and neither are the tasks AI agents need to solve. This is where adaptability comes into play—because no amount of past experience is going to help if the agent is thrown into an entirely new environment with unfamiliar challenges. It's like being dropped into a new city with no GPS. Sure, you've traveled before, but this time, the streets are different, the traffic patterns are new, and the roads are under construction.

Let's take the example of autonomous vehicles. An autonomous car is trained to navigate roads using experience-based learning from vast amounts of data—things like street signs, road conditions, and traffic flow. However, in real life, the environment can change unexpectedly: road construction, unpredictable drivers, sudden weather changes, and so on. An adaptable AI agent needs to recognize these changes and adjust its behavior accordingly.

One important feature of adaptability is the ability to generalize knowledge from past experiences. If an AI agent has learned how to perform a specific task in one setting, it should be able to apply that knowledge to a similar, but slightly different, setting. This is called transfer learning. For instance, if an AI agent trained to play one type of video game is transferred to another game with similar mechanics, it should be able to use its learned strategies and adapt them to the new game environment, even if it's never seen that specific game before.

Experience-Based Learning and Real-World Tasks

Experience-based learning isn't just for games—it's a crucial part of many real-world AI applications. For example, in healthcare, AI agents can use experience-based learning to diagnose diseases, recommend treatments, or even predict patient outcomes. The more the system interacts with medical data (e.g., patient histories, lab results, treatment responses), the better it becomes at identifying patterns and providing recommendations. However, this also requires a level of adaptability, as medical conditions can change, new diseases emerge, and patients react differently to treatments.

In robotics, an AI agent needs to be able to adapt to the dynamic physical environment it's working in. Robots that perform tasks in warehouses, for instance, must continuously adapt to changes in their surroundings, such as the movement of people or changes in the arrangement of goods. This adaptability allows the robots to keep working efficiently, even if the environment is constantly changing.

The same adaptability is crucial in industries like finance, where AI agents learn to make predictions based on stock market trends. However, since the stock market is constantly changing (thanks to news, global events, etc.), the AI agents need to adapt their strategies and decision-making processes in real-time. This makes experience-based learning a vital component of financial AI systems that can respond to the unpredictable nature of markets.

The Role of Feedback

At the heart of experience-based learning is the concept of feedback. Feedback helps the agent understand how well its actions align with its goals. In reinforcement learning, this feedback takes the form of rewards or penalties. For example, if an agent takes an action that leads to a positive outcome, it gets a reward (think of it as a "high five!"). If it makes a mistake, it gets a penalty (cue the sad trombone).

Positive feedback reinforces good behavior, motivating the agent to repeat that action, while negative feedback helps the agent understand what to avoid. Over time, the agent learns to maximize its rewards and minimize its penalties, improving its performance and becoming more efficient in its tasks.

The beauty of this system is that feedback can be delayed, which mimics real-life learning. For instance, you might not immediately know if your decision to skip your morning coffee was a good one, but after a few hours of feeling sluggish, you'll know for sure! AI agents rely on feedback over time to understand which actions contribute to success.

Conclusion: Learning as a Journey

Adaptability and experience-based learning are two key pillars of intelligent AI systems. Without these qualities, AI would be stuck in the stone age, unable to handle the ever-changing real world. By learning from its mistakes, improving over time, and adapting to new challenges, an AI agent can become an effective problem-solver capable of tackling complex, dynamic environments. In the end, it's not about how much data you have, but how well you can learn from that data and adapt. So next time you see an AI in action, just remember: it didn't get there overnight. It's been learning, adapting, and getting better, one experience at a time.

8.3 Feedback Loops and Performance Evaluation

In the world of AI, feedback loops are one of the most powerful tools for improvement. You've heard the phrase "trial and error" before, right? Well, that's essentially what feedback loops are—AI agents go through cycles of action, receive feedback, and adjust their behavior accordingly. But here's the catch: it's not just about making mistakes and trying again. It's about evaluating performance, identifying patterns, and tweaking actions to get better and better. Imagine you're learning how to bake the perfect cake. The first batch is a disaster, but after each attempt, you adjust the recipe slightly based on feedback—whether it's from the taste test or the way the cake rises. With each adjustment, you get closer to that mouth-watering cake, and by the end, you've mastered it. That's the feedback loop in action.

Feedback loops work in the same way for AI. After the agent performs an action, it receives feedback—which could be a reward (yay, the agent did something right) or a penalty (oops, that wasn't the best move). The agent then evaluates this feedback, updates its understanding, and adjusts its behavior to improve future actions. The entire process is iterative: each cycle of action, feedback, and adjustment leads to better decision-making and performance. This is especially important in dynamic, complex environments where the best solution is often learned over time, not all at once. Without feedback loops, an agent would be like a student who never gets graded—how would it ever know if it's improving?

The Anatomy of a Feedback Loop

At its core, a feedback loop follows a simple formula: action → feedback → adjustment → action → feedback → adjustment, and so on. But let's break it down in more detail.

Action: The agent performs an action based on its current knowledge or policy. For example, in a game, this could be choosing to move in a certain direction, or in a self-driving car, it might be steering left or right.

Feedback: After the action, the agent receives feedback. This could be a positive reward, a negative penalty, or some sort of metric that indicates how well the action aligned with the desired goal. The feedback could come in the form of points in a game, a change in a robot's position, or a financial reward in a stock-trading algorithm.

Adjustment: Based on the feedback, the agent adjusts its behavior. If the feedback was positive (yay!), the agent is likely to repeat that action in similar situations. If the feedback was negative (boo!), the agent will try to learn from the mistake and adjust its approach. This process is where learning happens. Over time, the agent's actions improve as it becomes better at maximizing rewards and minimizing penalties.

Performance Evaluation: Here's where we evaluate how well the agent is doing. Is it getting closer to its goals? How much has it improved over time? In real life, you can evaluate performance in terms of accuracy, efficiency, or success rate. But for AI agents, performance evaluation is often based on metrics like reward scores, accuracy rates, or completion times. Performance evaluation helps the agent determine if it's on the right track or needs to make further adjustments.

Feedback Loops in Action: Real-World Examples

To really understand how feedback loops work, let's look at a few examples.

Reinforcement Learning (RL): One of the most well-known applications of feedback loops is reinforcement learning, where an AI agent learns through interaction with its environment. For example, imagine training a robot to pick up objects in a warehouse.

Initially, the robot might fumble around, not knowing what to do. It receives feedback in the form of success or failure—if it successfully picks up an object, it gets a reward; if it fails, it gets a penalty. Over time, the robot learns which actions lead to success and adjusts its behavior accordingly, improving its performance with each iteration.

Self-Driving Cars: In the world of autonomous driving, feedback loops are crucial. A self-driving car constantly receives feedback from its sensors, such as cameras, radar, and LIDAR, to evaluate its surroundings. If it drives too close to a curb, the system adjusts, steering the car away to prevent collision. Similarly, when the car follows traffic laws and avoids obstacles, it receives positive feedback, further refining its driving abilities.

E-commerce Recommendations: Online shopping sites like Amazon or Netflix use feedback loops to improve their recommendations. The more you interact with the system—by watching movies, adding items to your cart, or clicking on recommendations—the more the system learns about your preferences. The feedback it receives (whether you buy the item or not, whether you watch the movie to the end or skip it) helps it adjust future recommendations to be more aligned with your interests.

Evaluating Performance: The Secret Sauce

Now, let's talk about performance evaluation. Without performance evaluation, feedback loops would be like playing darts in the dark—you wouldn't know if you're hitting the target or just missing the board completely. So how do we evaluate performance?

In the simplest terms, performance evaluation measures how well the agent is achieving its goals. For example:

Accuracy: How close is the agent's output to the correct or desired outcome? For a self-driving car, accuracy could mean staying in the lane and following the traffic rules correctly.

Efficiency: How quickly and effectively is the agent accomplishing its task? In a stock-trading system, this could be how quickly the agent responds to market fluctuations and makes profitable trades.

Reward maximization: In reinforcement learning, the primary goal is often to maximize rewards. An agent's performance can be evaluated based on how well it's able to optimize its actions to maximize long-term rewards while minimizing penalties.

Performance evaluation isn't just about checking whether an agent is "right" or "wrong." It's a nuanced process of assessing how well the agent's actions align with its objectives, and where it can improve. Often, performance is measured using metrics such as accuracy rates, success rates, or reward scores. These metrics tell the story of how far the agent has come and what it still needs to work on.

Why Feedback Loops Matter

Feedback loops are the lifeblood of AI performance. They allow agents to learn from their environment, adapt their behavior, and improve over time. Without these loops, AI agents would be static, predictable, and, frankly, a bit dumb. So, whether we're talking about a robot in a warehouse, a self-driving car, or your favorite Netflix recommendation system, feedback loops play a huge role in making sure these agents can learn, adapt, and improve.

By constantly evaluating and adjusting based on feedback, AI agents evolve and get closer to performing tasks like a pro. As with everything, it's all about the cycle—action, feedback, adjustment—and then doing it all over again, better than before. It's like riding a bike; the more you practice (with feedback), the more confident you become. And, spoiler alert, the same goes for AI agents.

So next time you see an AI doing something impressive, just remember: it's not magic—it's the power of feedback loops and performance evaluation working their behind-the-scenes wonders!

8.4 Incorporating External Knowledge Sources

When it comes to making AI agents smarter, it's pretty much like teaching a dog a trick. Sure, you can train them with a set of instructions, but sometimes, it helps if they can get a little extra knowledge to level up their skills. That's where external knowledge sources come into play. Instead of relying solely on internal programming and data, agents can tap into vast pools of external data to expand their capabilities and decision-making power. You know how you Google something when you don't know the answer? AI agents can do the same thing, except they're faster and never forget what they read. By incorporating these external sources—whether it's databases, expert systems, internet resources, or even the collective wisdom of other agents—AI becomes a bit of a knowledge sponge. And believe me, they soak up information faster than I can finish my morning coffee!

Now, to get down to the technical side of things—what does it actually mean for an AI agent to incorporate external knowledge? Well, AI systems can access and integrate various external sources, such as expert databases, public knowledge bases (think Wikipedia), domain-specific resources, and even real-time information from online services. These sources act as a sort of "booster" for the agent, allowing it to process and apply more data, making more informed decisions. It's like adding a cheat code to the agent's brain that gives it supercharged knowledge in specific areas.

Types of External Knowledge Sources

There are several ways AI agents can tap into external knowledge sources. It's not just about pulling random data out of thin air—there's a method to the madness. Some common sources include:

Databases: Structured data repositories like SQL databases or cloud-based data warehouses are rich sources of factual knowledge. For instance, an AI agent in a medical application might access a medical database to check for symptoms, diagnoses, and treatments. These databases are often curated and continually updated, ensuring that the agent has access to the most relevant and up-to-date information.

Knowledge Graphs: These are graphical representations of knowledge, often used in natural language processing (NLP) and search engines. They capture relationships between concepts. For example, Google uses a knowledge graph to enhance search results by connecting related pieces of information. An AI agent could tap into such a graph to understand context, connections, and semantics better.

Expert Systems: Expert systems are specialized AI programs that emulate the decision-making ability of a human expert in a particular field. For instance, an AI agent used in legal document analysis might pull information from a legal expert system to interpret complex laws and regulations. These expert systems are designed to simulate human expertise, and they provide valuable insights to agents who lack domain-specific knowledge.

Crowdsourced Data: AI agents can also benefit from crowdsourced knowledge—think Wikipedia, Reddit threads, or even specialized forums. This type of data is constantly evolving as more people contribute their knowledge and experiences. A great example is how some conversational agents, like chatbots, use crowdsourced FAQ data to help them answer customer queries.

Sensor Networks: In some cases, AI agents can access external information in real time from sensor networks. These could be from the internet of things (IoT) devices, weather stations, or even traffic data. For example, a smart city AI agent might incorporate real-time traffic data from sensor networks to optimize traffic flow and improve navigation for drivers.

Online Resources: Online APIs (application programming interfaces) provide a treasure trove of external knowledge that AI agents can use. For example, integrating an AI agent with Google Maps API allows the agent to pull up-to-date location data, while an AI that works with financial markets might tap into stock market APIs to receive real-time trading information.

Social Media and User-Generated Content: Social media platforms like Twitter and Facebook generate massive amounts of data daily. While unstructured and sometimes messy, this type of information can be valuable for AI agents when it comes to real-time trends, sentiment analysis, and consumer behavior.

How External Knowledge Improves AI Agent Performance

Now, you might be wondering: "Okay, this all sounds great, but how exactly does incorporating external knowledge help my AI agent be better at its job?" Great question! Here's how:

Context Awareness: By pulling in external data, AI agents can gain more context. Instead of relying on static data or pre-programmed rules, they can adjust their responses and behaviors based on real-time input. For example, if an AI agent is trying to recommend movies to a user, it can pull data from streaming platforms, user reviews, and even trending topics on social media to make more personalized suggestions.

Enhanced Decision-Making: Imagine an AI agent that's trying to predict stock prices. If it only uses historical stock data to make decisions, it might miss out on more timely factors, like changes in market sentiment or global events. By pulling in external sources like news feeds or economic reports, the AI can make more informed decisions that lead to better outcomes.

Learning from Diverse Sources: When AI agents incorporate external knowledge, they're not just learning from one dataset—they're learning from a broad spectrum of information. This enables them to be more adaptable and flexible. Think of it like a student who's learning from multiple textbooks, not just one. The more diverse the sources, the better-rounded the agent's knowledge becomes.

Problem-Solving and Optimization: In some cases, external knowledge can directly help AI agents solve complex problems. Take optimization algorithms as an example. By feeding external data like geographic maps or real-time weather patterns, an AI agent could find the fastest route for a delivery truck or optimize the timing of a manufacturing process to account for changes in raw material supply.

Real-World Examples of External Knowledge Integration

Let's look at how incorporating external knowledge works in real-world AI systems:

AI in Healthcare: In a medical diagnosis system, an AI agent could access external knowledge sources like medical research papers, drug databases, and clinical trial results. This would enable it to make better recommendations about diagnoses or treatments based on the latest available information.

Virtual Assistants (like Siri or Alexa): These systems rely heavily on external knowledge sources, like weather forecasts, traffic updates, and news articles. They can pull real-time data to answer queries accurately—whether it's telling you the weather or giving you the latest stock market updates.

Smart Manufacturing: In industrial applications, AI agents can integrate data from IoT sensors to monitor machinery health and optimize production schedules. They might also use external resources, like predictive maintenance algorithms or supply chain databases, to improve efficiency.

Challenges and Considerations

Of course, integrating external knowledge isn't without its challenges. There are a few things to keep in mind:

Data Quality: Not all external sources are created equal. For an AI agent to make the best use of external data, that data needs to be reliable, accurate, and up-to-date. Garbage in, garbage out, as they say!

Complexity and Overload: Too much external information can overwhelm an AI system. It's important to ensure that the agent only pulls in the relevant data, or it risks drowning in an ocean of unnecessary information.

Data Privacy: External knowledge sources often contain sensitive information, especially in areas like healthcare and finance. It's critical to ensure that any external data used is in compliance with privacy regulations and ethical standards.

Wrapping Up

Incorporating external knowledge sources is like giving your AI agent a library card to the world. Instead of just learning from its own experiences, it can tap into the collective knowledge available outside its environment. By combining internal processing with external data, agents become smarter, more adaptable, and better equipped to handle complex tasks.

So, the next time you see an AI agent acing a task, just remember: it didn't get there on its own. It had a little help from the vast, interconnected web of data out there—and it's all the better for it!

8.5 Continuous and Lifelong Learning in Agents

AI agents, much like humans, don't just stop learning once they get the basics down. Sure, they can be incredibly intelligent out of the gate, but the real magic happens when they continue to learn and adapt over time. This concept of continuous and lifelong learning is where AI agents start to shine. In a world that's constantly changing—new trends, data, and even technology appearing every day—AI agents need to be just as dynamic as their environment. If they were to stop learning, they'd be like that one guy at the party who never updates his playlist—kind of out of touch and a bit stale.

Continuous learning refers to the process where AI agents continually absorb new information and experiences, adjusting their behavior and knowledge base as they go. Unlike traditional models that might be trained once and then set aside, agents designed with continuous learning can keep improving throughout their operational life. Think about it this way: an AI agent could learn about changes in a user's preferences, new types of data emerging in its domain, or even entirely new technologies that require adaptation. It's like upgrading from an old flip phone to the latest smartphone, but in the world of AI, it happens automatically and in real time. Imagine an AI agent in healthcare, for example, continuously learning from new medical research, patient data, and treatment outcomes—constantly improving its diagnostic capabilities and recommendations over time. Now that's a powerful, adaptable agent.

The Importance of Lifelong Learning in AI

To understand why lifelong learning is so crucial, consider how we, as humans, learn. We don't just learn things once and then call it a day. Our experiences over time shape who we are and what we know. Lifelong learning in AI is essentially the same thing. It's about the agent acquiring knowledge not just once, but over its entire life, learning from every action, interaction, and data point it encounters. For an agent to be truly effective, it needs to continuously refine its behavior, improve its performance, and adapt to the complexities of its environment.

Let's say you have an AI agent built to recommend movies. Initially, it knows a little bit about the types of films you like based on the data it's been trained on. But over time, the agent starts to observe your changing tastes, the types of movies you now enjoy, and maybe even preferences you didn't realize you had. The more data it gets, the smarter it becomes at predicting what you'll love next. This lifelong learning enables the agent to remain relevant and useful, no matter how much your tastes evolve. And the best part? It doesn't require manual updates or retraining—it does it all by itself.

The Two Pillars of Lifelong Learning: Adaptation and Improvement

There are two main components to continuous and lifelong learning in agents: adaptation and improvement. Let's break them down.

Adaptation: This is the ability of an agent to adjust to new data and situations that it may not have encountered during its initial training. Adaptation ensures that the agent is not just relying on static knowledge, but actively adjusting its models and strategies based on new experiences. For instance, if an AI agent that's controlling a robot suddenly encounters an obstacle it wasn't programmed for, adaptation means that the robot can alter its behavior in real-time to deal with the obstacle. It doesn't need a complete overhaul; it just adapts and continues forward.

Improvement: Over time, an agent should improve its performance. This is not just about handling new scenarios, but also about becoming better at what it was originally designed to do. For example, a personal assistant AI that learns to recognize more intricate details about its user, or a self-driving car that gets more efficient at navigating complex traffic situations. The key here is that improvement doesn't stop. As the agent encounters more data, it should find more effective ways to achieve its goals.

Together, adaptation and improvement create an agent that is not just reactive, but proactively bettering itself, becoming more proficient with each new piece of information or each new task it encounters.

Techniques for Lifelong Learning in AI Agents

So, how do we make sure that AI agents can keep learning and improving over time? There are a few key techniques that help agents achieve lifelong learning:

Incremental Learning: This technique allows AI agents to update their knowledge gradually without losing past learning. It's like adding new chapters to a book without erasing the old ones. This is particularly useful in environments where the data is constantly changing, such as e-commerce or social media platforms, where new trends and products emerge all the time. Incremental learning ensures that the agent doesn't forget its past knowledge while learning something new.

Online Learning: This is the ability for an agent to learn in real-time. Online learning is especially important when an agent needs to adapt to rapidly changing environments. For example, imagine a stock market trading bot that learns new market trends on the fly—without waiting for a large batch of new data to be processed. Online learning allows the agent to continuously incorporate new information as it arrives, helping it stay up-to-date.

Transfer Learning: Transfer learning allows an agent to take knowledge learned from one task and apply it to another, related task. This makes it possible for agents to generalize knowledge and apply it to different domains. For example, an agent trained to recognize animals in pictures can transfer its learned skills to identify other objects, like cars or trees, by leveraging what it's already learned about visual patterns.

Self-Supervised Learning: This method allows agents to learn without needing explicit supervision. It's like learning from your mistakes. In self-supervised learning, agents create their own labels or tasks from the raw data they encounter. Over time, they refine their understanding of patterns and structures. This method is particularly powerful because it enables the agent to learn continuously without needing human intervention every step of the way.

Challenges of Lifelong Learning in AI

Of course, no great system comes without its challenges. Continuous and lifelong learning in AI agents isn't a walk in the park, and there are a few hurdles we need to overcome.

Catastrophic Forgetting: This is the tendency of AI agents to forget previously learned information when new data is introduced. If an AI agent is constantly learning, it can sometimes "overwrite" old knowledge with new data, leading to the loss of valuable insights. This is especially problematic when the agent needs to retain knowledge for long-term tasks. Researchers are constantly working on ways to prevent this from happening by developing better learning algorithms and methods for "remembering" what the agent has learned.

Data Quality and Consistency: In lifelong learning, the quality of the data is incredibly important. Poor or inconsistent data can lead the agent to make incorrect assumptions or decisions. Ensuring that the agent is exposed to high-quality, consistent data is key to its success in continuous learning.

Computational Resources: Lifelong learning requires ongoing processing and storage of data, which can be resource-intensive. For AI systems deployed in resource-constrained environments, like on-device agents or mobile robots, continuous learning might be difficult without sufficient computational power and storage capacity.

Conclusion

In the end, continuous and lifelong learning in AI agents is what will truly set them apart in the long run. It allows agents to adapt, improve, and evolve with time, keeping them relevant in ever-changing environments. By incorporating techniques like incremental learning, transfer learning, and online learning, agents can not only perform better but also tackle more complex tasks. The future of AI lies in agents that don't just execute commands but grow, improve, and learn from every interaction and experience. And let's face it—if they can do that, who wouldn't want one around?

Chapter 9: Applications of AI Agents

AI agents aren't just living in the lab anymore—they've escaped into your phone, your car, and probably your smart fridge. This chapter is where things get real. From helpful assistants to cunning game opponents, we tour the world of AI agents already embedded in daily life, doing everything from making recommendations to beating humans at board games.

This chapter surveys practical applications of AI agents across various domains. Topics include virtual assistants and smart home systems, industrial automation, gaming, scientific research, and emerging technologies. Case studies highlight how agents are applied in different sectors and explore trends shaping future applications.

9.1 AI Agents in Daily Life (Smart Homes, Virtual Assistants)

Alright, picture this: you wake up in the morning, and your smart speaker greets you like an old friend, saying, "Good morning! Your coffee is brewing, and traffic's light today." Sounds like the future, right? Well, guess what? This isn't some distant sci-fi dream. It's your AI-powered smart home in action, doing what it does best—making your life easier without you even having to ask. From smart thermostats that know the perfect temperature for your comfort to virtual assistants that handle everything from your calendar to your grocery list, AI agents are becoming the quiet but powerful heroes of our daily lives.

In a world where we're all trying to juggle work, social lives, and the occasional existential crisis (we've all been there), having an AI agent around is like having an ultra-efficient personal assistant on call 24/7. Whether it's setting reminders, adjusting lighting, controlling security systems, or even making dinner suggestions, AI agents are the trusty sidekicks we never knew we needed. Sure, they might not make you breakfast in bed (yet), but they're pretty darn close.

AI Agents in Smart Homes

The concept of a smart home is rapidly becoming a staple of modern living, and at the heart of this transformation are AI agents. They help manage everything from heating and lighting to security and entertainment systems. Imagine walking into your house after a long day, and your smart home agent automatically dims the lights, adjusts the temperature to your preferred setting, and even plays your favorite playlist without you lifting a finger. This is AI making your home feel like a personalized, efficient haven.

But it's not just about comfort—AI agents in smart homes play a significant role in energy efficiency and safety too. Take a smart thermostat, for example. It learns your schedule over time, turning the heat down when you're at work and warming the house up before you come back, all while reducing energy consumption. Similarly, smart security systems powered by AI can learn patterns in your behavior, detect unusual activity, and alert you to potential security threats before you even realize something's wrong. It's like having an invisible, ever-vigilant guardian for your home.

Virtual Assistants: Your New Best Friend

Then there are virtual assistants—your digital sidekick who's always there when you need them. Whether it's Siri, Alexa, Google Assistant, or even the less-known ones, these AI agents are designed to make your life easier. They're capable of doing a lot more than just telling you the weather or setting alarms (though they do those things pretty darn well). These agents can send text messages, play music, set reminders, control other smart devices, and answer almost any random question you throw at them. You could say they're the Swiss Army knives of the AI world—ready to help with whatever you need, no matter how big or small.

But virtual assistants aren't just for the home. They're also integrated into many modern smartphones, cars, and wearables, offering hands-free assistance wherever you go. Need to send a quick message while driving? Ask your assistant. Want to find the best pizza place nearby? Ask away. It's like having a mini-me in your pocket, always ready to assist, entertain, or even argue with you about what song you should listen to next (because let's be honest, we've all had those "music fights" with our assistants).

The AI Learning Curve

What makes these AI agents truly remarkable is their ability to learn and adapt. Virtual assistants and smart home systems don't just follow a rigid set of rules—they improve over time. They observe your preferences, adjust to your habits, and offer smarter suggestions based on past interactions. This learning process makes them more efficient and personalized as time goes on. For instance, an AI assistant might start recommending new music based on what you've previously listened to or suggest tasks that match your usual routine.

But the real kicker? They're not just reactive—they're predictive. For example, if you always have a cup of coffee in the morning and then check your calendar for the day, your smart assistant might start proactively suggesting coffee from your favorite café or even pulling up your schedule as soon as it detects you're up. It's like they're starting to read your mind (creepy? maybe a little—but also incredibly useful).

Challenges and Privacy Concerns

Now, before you get too excited about handing over full control to these little AI marvels, there are some important challenges and concerns we need to address. One of the most significant issues is privacy. AI agents are constantly collecting data to improve their recommendations and services. They learn from your behavior, interactions, and habits, which raises questions about how that data is stored and protected. It's crucial that we maintain control over our personal data and ensure that the systems we use are transparent about how they handle it.

Additionally, while AI agents can learn and adapt, there's still room for improvement in communication. For instance, if you have a smart home system and you ask it to "set the lights to mood lighting," it might not always interpret your request the way you expect. This can lead to frustrating moments when your perfectly crafted command is met with confusion. As AI systems evolve, these misinterpretations will become fewer, but for now, expect a bit of trial and error.

The Future: More AI, More Efficiency, More Fun

Looking to the future, the potential for AI agents in our daily lives is boundless. As these systems become more sophisticated, their integration into various aspects of our daily routines will only grow. We're talking about intelligent homes that respond to your emotions (based on your voice or even facial expressions), AI-powered health assistants that track your well-being, and even virtual assistants who help you plan your social life as effectively as they manage your calendar.

The real question isn't whether AI agents will become a part of our daily lives—they already have. It's how far we're willing to let them go. Sure, there's a lot of excitement around AI agents making things more convenient, but the future holds even greater potential for personalized experiences, efficiency, and yes—maybe even a bit of fun.

So next time you talk to your virtual assistant or adjust your thermostat, just know this: you're not just interacting with a device—you're engaging with an evolving, learning AI agent that's working hard to make your life a little easier, one smart decision at a time. How cool is that?

9.2 AI Agents in Business and Industry

Imagine walking into your office one morning and finding that your AI assistant has already reviewed your emails, scheduled your meetings, and even drafted some reports for you. You didn't have to lift a finger—your AI agent had it all covered. While this might sound like something out of a futuristic sci-fi movie, it's actually happening right now in businesses and industries all over the world. From chatbots handling customer service to intelligent systems optimizing supply chains, AI agents are no longer just a cool concept— they're essential tools that drive productivity, efficiency, and innovation.

In business, the game has changed. Companies are no longer relying solely on humans to manage repetitive tasks or make data-driven decisions. Instead, AI agents are being employed to do the heavy lifting. They're automating everything from inventory management and fraud detection to marketing campaigns and financial forecasting. And let's not forget about the customer experience—AI-powered chatbots are now handling millions of customer queries every day, delivering faster responses, fewer mistakes, and sometimes even a touch of personality. In industries ranging from healthcare and finance to manufacturing and retail, AI agents are reshaping how things are done, often behind the scenes, making the whole machine of business run smoother, smarter, and faster.

AI in Customer Service: Chatbots and Virtual Assistants

One of the most visible and popular uses of AI agents in business is in customer service. Have you ever chatted with a customer service bot and been surprised by how well it understood your issue? Or perhaps you've received that perfectly timed reminder from your virtual assistant about an upcoming meeting or bill? That's AI in action, and it's everywhere. Companies are leveraging AI agents to automate customer interactions, saving time and providing more efficient service.

Chatbots are among the most commonly used AI agents in business. They're being used by companies like Amazon, banks, and telecom providers to answer frequently asked questions, troubleshoot common problems, and even guide customers through purchasing processes. By handling routine inquiries, AI-powered chatbots free up human agents to focus on more complex or sensitive issues. But that's not all. As these systems learn from their interactions, they become better and more capable of addressing customer needs, often predicting what a customer will need before they even ask. It's like having a team of invisible customer service agents working around the clock to keep things running smoothly.

AI in Supply Chain and Operations

Beyond customer service, AI agents are also making significant strides in supply chain management and operations optimization. Imagine this: a warehouse that runs itself. AI agents can track inventory, predict demand, and even optimize delivery routes to ensure that products get to customers in record time. Companies are now using AI to predict when to restock products, which suppliers will provide the best deals, and how to streamline operations for maximum efficiency.

In fact, major retailers like Walmart and e-commerce giants like Amazon have already integrated AI-powered systems into their supply chains. These systems use machine learning algorithms to predict trends in product demand, reducing waste and ensuring that companies can meet customer needs faster and more accurately. AI agents are even being deployed in logistics to calculate the most efficient shipping routes and ensure that products arrive on time, saving money and improving overall customer satisfaction.

AI in Financial Services

The financial sector is another area where AI agents are making waves. With the rise of algorithmic trading, fraud detection, and risk analysis, financial institutions are increasingly turning to AI to handle tasks that once required teams of analysts. AI agents are used to process massive amounts of financial data in real time, identify trends, and make predictions with far more accuracy than human traders could ever hope to achieve.

AI agents in fraud detection are particularly important, as they can quickly analyze patterns in transaction data and flag suspicious activity. These agents can work around the clock, learning from new data to detect previously unseen patterns, helping financial institutions prevent fraud before it happens. Similarly, AI is being used in investment strategies to predict market fluctuations and help firms make smarter investment decisions. It's like having a financial advisor that never sleeps, never takes a vacation, and always has the most up-to-date market knowledge at its fingertips.

AI in Marketing and Customer Insights

If you've ever felt like your favorite brand knows you a little too well, chances are it's thanks to AI. Businesses are now using AI agents to gather customer insights, predict purchasing behavior, and personalize marketing strategies. These systems analyze past purchases, online behavior, and even social media activity to create highly personalized experiences for customers. From targeted ads to customized product recommendations, AI agents are helping businesses build stronger, more engaging relationships with their customers.

These agents don't just stop at creating personalized experiences. They also help businesses understand market trends, track competitor activity, and identify new opportunities. With the ability to analyze massive datasets, AI agents can predict what products or services will be most popular, allowing companies to stay one step ahead of the competition. It's not magic—it's just AI working its predictive powers, and businesses are taking full advantage of it.

AI in Healthcare and Diagnostics

The healthcare industry is also experiencing a revolution, thanks to AI agents. These systems are being used to assist with diagnostics, treatment recommendations, and even patient monitoring. AI agents can analyze medical data, such as patient records, medical images, and genetic information, to identify potential health issues that might be missed by human doctors. They are even capable of assisting with drug discovery, speeding up the process of finding new treatments and medications.

For example, in radiology, AI agents can scan medical images like X-rays and MRIs to detect abnormalities, such as tumors or fractures, with greater accuracy than human radiologists in some cases. In patient care, AI agents can monitor vital signs, track medications, and provide real-time updates to healthcare providers. These systems can even predict potential health problems based on historical data, allowing doctors to intervene before issues become critical.

The Challenges and Future of AI in Business

While the potential of AI in business is immense, there are still challenges to overcome. Data privacy and security concerns are at the forefront, especially when AI systems have access to sensitive customer and financial data. Additionally, integrating AI into legacy systems can be complex and costly, requiring significant upfront investment. Businesses also need to ensure that their AI agents are transparent, ethical, and unbiased in their decision-making processes.

Looking ahead, the future of AI in business is bright. As AI agents become more sophisticated, they'll take on even more responsibilities, from automating entire workflows to providing advanced decision support. Businesses that embrace AI and integrate these systems into their operations will gain a competitive edge, becoming more efficient, innovative, and responsive to customer needs.

AI agents in business and industry are transforming the way companies operate and interact with customers. From automating routine tasks to making critical decisions, these agents are making businesses smarter, more efficient, and more adaptable. While challenges remain, the opportunities for growth and innovation are vast. For companies willing to invest in AI, the future is filled with exciting possibilities. AI agents aren't just the future—they're here, and they're already making a huge impact. So, buckle up, because this AI revolution is just getting started!

9.3 Agents in Gaming and Entertainment

Let's face it: who doesn't love a good game? Whether it's slaying dragons in a fantasy world or racing at breakneck speeds down virtual highways, video games offer an escape to an alternate universe—one where your only job is to beat the boss or get to the next level. But have you ever wondered how game developers make it all come together? How do they create those incredibly smart non-playable characters (NPCs) who can outwit you, taunt you, or even team up with you? The secret behind all that is none other than the AI agents that drive the behavior and actions of game characters. These agents aren't just mindlessly following scripts—they're smart, adaptable, and capable of creating truly immersive experiences that feel almost... human.

From your trusty sidekick who follows you on your quest to the hostile enemies that keep you on your toes, AI agents are what give a game its depth and excitement. But beyond gaming, AI agents are also making waves in entertainment as a whole—helping to create more personalized content, enhance viewer experiences, and even assist in content creation. So, if you think gaming is just about pressing buttons and following a storyline, think again. The power of AI agents is shaping the future of how we play, watch, and experience entertainment in ways we're only beginning to understand.

AI Agents in Video Games

In the world of video games, AI agents are responsible for controlling everything from enemy behavior to the actions of NPCs. In the past, game developers would rely on pre-written scripts to dictate how characters would behave. While that worked for a while, it didn't exactly allow for dynamic, lifelike interactions. Enter AI agents—these smart little systems now control NPC behavior, enabling them to adapt to player actions and create more realistic, unpredictable gaming experiences.

Take first-person shooters, for example. In these games, AI agents control the enemies you face. Instead of simply charging at you in a straight line, these agents will analyze the situation, take cover, communicate with other enemies, and react based on your actions. If you're hiding behind a barricade, they might throw a grenade or flank your position. It's like playing chess with opponents who never make the same move twice—keeping you on your toes and adding to the overall challenge. These AI-driven characters are also capable of learning and adapting their tactics over time, ensuring that the game never feels too easy or too repetitive.

But it's not just the bad guys that benefit from AI. Companion characters in games like The Last of Us or Halo are controlled by AI agents, which makes them seem more like real allies. These agents can assist you by providing cover fire, offering advice, or even interacting with you through dialogue. They learn from your actions and make decisions based on the context, making for a more engaging experience.

The Evolution of AI in Gaming

The use of AI agents in gaming has evolved drastically over the years. In the early days, AI was simple and could only follow basic decision trees. Characters would repeat the same actions every time, making games predictable and often dull. However, with the rise of machine learning and more sophisticated algorithms, AI agents in modern games are capable of much more complex behaviors.

Today's AI agents are designed to make gaming experiences more immersive and dynamic. Games like Red Dead Redemption 2 or Grand Theft Auto V feature NPCs that go about their daily routines in the game world—buying coffee, chatting with each other, or even going to work. This level of detail creates a more vibrant, believable world, where the characters seem like they have their own lives beyond the player's interaction.

Not only are AI agents getting better at mimicking human behavior, but they're also becoming more intuitive, responding to players' emotional states and changing tactics accordingly. Some AI agents are even capable of recognizing patterns in a player's gameplay and adjusting their behavior to either challenge or help them. For example, if a player consistently struggles with a particular task, the AI might offer subtle hints or adjust the difficulty level.

AI in Interactive Storytelling and Virtual Worlds

In addition to their role in gameplay, AI agents are also transforming the storytelling aspect of gaming. Games like The Witcher 3 or Mass Effect allow players to make choices that affect the storyline, but it's the AI agents behind these narratives that ensure those choices have real consequences. These AI-driven systems manage complex branching storylines, dynamically adjusting events and outcomes based on player decisions.

Moreover, AI agents are playing a significant role in the development of virtual worlds and augmented reality experiences. Imagine a game where the world itself changes based on your interactions, and the AI agents who populate it learn from the decisions you make. These virtual worlds become more reactive, alive, and ever-evolving, keeping players engaged for hours. The more you explore, the more the game adapts to your choices, creating a truly unique experience every time you play.

AI in Entertainment Beyond Gaming

It's not just the gaming world where AI agents are having an impact—entertainment as a whole is also being reshaped by AI. From personalized content recommendations to AI-driven film scripts, these agents are changing the way we consume and create media.

For example, streaming services like Netflix or Spotify rely heavily on AI agents to recommend shows, movies, and music based on your tastes. These AI agents analyze your past viewing or listening behavior, understand your preferences, and suggest content that you're likely to enjoy. The more you interact with the system, the better it gets at predicting what will keep you hooked.

But the influence of AI doesn't stop there. In the world of content creation, AI is being used to generate music, art, and even scripts for films and TV shows. While this might sound like something straight out of a sci-fi dystopia, it's already happening. AI-driven algorithms are capable of analyzing existing content, understanding the key components that make it popular, and using that knowledge to create new, original works. Of course, this doesn't mean that robots are taking over the creative industry (at least, not yet). Instead, AI is acting as a tool that complements and enhances human creativity, allowing artists to push boundaries and create in new ways.

The Future of AI in Gaming and Entertainment

As the technology continues to advance, the potential for AI agents in both gaming and entertainment is practically limitless. In the future, we might see AI agents that are even more capable of creating immersive, interactive experiences—from virtual reality games where every NPC has a personality and backstory to AI-driven films where the audience's choices influence the plot in real-time.

One of the most exciting developments in the world of AI-powered entertainment is the possibility of personalized, adaptive experiences. Imagine watching a movie where the plot changes depending on your emotional reactions, or playing a game where the story evolves as you make decisions. With AI agents, these kinds of experiences could soon be a reality.

AI agents are already playing a crucial role in shaping the future of gaming and entertainment. Whether they're controlling enemies, guiding players through quests, or helping create new content, these agents are making games and media more immersive, dynamic, and personalized. As AI technology continues to evolve, it's only a matter of time before we see even more groundbreaking innovations in these industries, making our experiences more exciting and interactive than ever before. So, get ready—because the next level of AI-driven entertainment is just around the corner!

9.4 Scientific Research and Data Exploration Agents

Let's talk about the thrill of discovery. The moment when you stumble upon something that changes everything, when you crack the code or uncover an answer that's been hiding in plain sight for decades. Now, imagine that instead of toiling away in the lab or pouring through mountains of research papers, you had an AI agent as your personal research assistant, tirelessly scouring through data, spotting patterns, and even suggesting the next step in your experiment. Sounds pretty amazing, right? Well, that's exactly what's happening today in the world of scientific research. AI agents are no longer just assistants—they're becoming full-fledged partners in discovery, transforming the way science is done.

Whether you're studying genetic sequences, simulating climate change, or diving into astrophysics, AI agents are helping scientists navigate vast data sets and conduct experiments with far more speed and accuracy than ever before. Think about it—while traditional research might have taken years or even decades to yield results, AI-powered agents can sift through massive amounts of data in a fraction of the time, making connections that humans might have missed. But AI's role isn't just limited to speeding up data processing; it's also enabling a new wave of predictive modeling, simulation, and even hypothesis generation. So, let's dive into how these clever agents are shaking up the world of scientific research and data exploration.

AI Agents in Scientific Discovery

In the past, scientific research relied heavily on human expertise and manual data processing. Researchers would often spend hours, days, or even months gathering data, running experiments, and analyzing results. With the rise of AI, all of this has changed. AI agents are now playing a pivotal role in speeding up the research process by automating data analysis, generating hypotheses, and even running experiments autonomously.

Take drug discovery as an example. Historically, developing new pharmaceuticals involved an immense amount of trial and error. Researchers would test hundreds, if not thousands, of compounds to find those that might work against a particular disease. Today, AI agents are helping accelerate this process by analyzing chemical structures, predicting how different molecules will interact, and identifying promising drug candidates much more efficiently. Deep learning algorithms have become particularly good at recognizing patterns in biological data, allowing researchers to uncover novel insights in diseases and treatments that would have been nearly impossible with traditional methods.

But AI's reach goes beyond just pharmaceuticals. AI-powered agents are also being used in genomic research to analyze DNA sequences. These agents can process vast amounts of genetic data to identify mutations, predict the risk of genetic diseases, and even help design personalized treatments for patients based on their genetic profiles. Researchers no longer have to rely solely on human analysis; AI is stepping in to help make sense of the overwhelming volume of data produced by modern sequencing technologies.

AI in Data Exploration and Predictive Modeling

One of the most significant contributions of AI agents to scientific research is in the realm of data exploration. Modern science generates an incredible amount of data—from particle collisions in physics experiments to environmental measurements in climate studies. Processing and analyzing this data manually is no longer feasible, and this is where AI steps in. AI agents can process data at speeds and scales that were previously unimaginable, helping researchers identify hidden patterns, generate insights, and even predict future outcomes.

In climate science, for example, AI agents are being used to analyze vast climate datasets, model weather patterns, and predict future climate changes. These agents can process data from satellite imagery, ocean temperatures, atmospheric conditions, and more, to create predictive models of climate behavior. By understanding these patterns, scientists can better anticipate extreme weather events, make informed decisions about policy, and improve long-term climate models.

Similarly, in astronomy, AI agents are being used to sift through terabytes of data from telescopes and satellites to discover new celestial bodies, identify anomalies, and even help classify galaxies. Machine learning models can spot patterns in images of the night sky that might be too subtle for the human eye, leading to new discoveries and a deeper understanding of the universe.

Automating Hypothesis Generation

What if an AI agent could generate hypotheses for you? Sounds like something out of a science fiction movie, but it's already happening. In traditional research, hypotheses are based on existing theories, prior knowledge, and observation. However, AI agents are now capable of synthesizing new ideas based on existing data, literature, and research findings.

In fields like material science, AI agents are helping researchers predict the properties of new materials before they've even been synthesized in the lab. By analyzing existing material data, AI can predict which combinations of elements are likely to result in materials with the desired properties, such as higher strength, improved conductivity, or better resistance to corrosion. These AI-driven predictions can save researchers months or even years of trial and error.

Similarly, AI agents in physics are helping generate hypotheses for new theories by combing through data and recognizing patterns that might lead to breakthroughs in quantum mechanics or theoretical physics. Rather than relying entirely on the scientific method or established paradigms, AI provides a fresh perspective, proposing novel ideas and solutions that researchers might not have considered.

Enhancing Simulations and Virtual Experiments

Another area where AI agents are making a massive impact is in the world of simulations and virtual experiments. Traditional physical experiments can be time-consuming, expensive, and sometimes dangerous. But with AI-powered simulations, scientists can model complex systems and run virtual experiments without ever stepping foot in a lab.

In particle physics, for example, AI agents are used to simulate subatomic particle collisions and predict outcomes based on different conditions. This allows physicists to test theories and refine models without needing to conduct every single experiment in a physical particle accelerator. Similarly, in biotechnology, AI is used to simulate the behavior of proteins and molecules in various environments, providing insights into how they might interact in the human body. This kind of predictive power is revolutionizing drug development and other biotechnological fields.

Collaboration Across Disciplines

One of the most exciting aspects of AI in scientific research is its ability to bridge disciplines and encourage collaborative innovation. Scientists in different fields can now work together more effectively by sharing AI-powered tools and techniques that help them analyze and interpret data in new ways. For example, biologists, chemists, and physicists can all use the same AI models to analyze complex datasets, share insights, and collaborate on solving grand challenges like curing diseases or addressing climate change.

AI agents also enable more global collaboration by making research findings more accessible and easier to share. Researchers from all over the world can upload their data to shared platforms, where AI systems help analyze the information and generate actionable insights. This opens up new possibilities for crowdsourced research and open science, where everyone can contribute to solving some of the world's biggest challenges.

The Future of AI in Scientific Research

Looking ahead, the potential for AI agents in scientific research is enormous. As these agents continue to evolve, they'll become even more adept at processing larger datasets, generating insights, and predicting outcomes. The integration of quantum computing with AI could unlock new levels of data analysis, enabling breakthroughs in everything from drug discovery to space exploration.

As AI technology advances, scientists will continue to rely on these agents to push the boundaries of knowledge, automate tedious tasks, and generate new ideas. The future of science is undoubtedly going to be driven by AI agents, helping to make sense of the universe in ways that were once unimaginable.

AI agents are transforming scientific research and data exploration, enabling researchers to process vast amounts of data, make faster discoveries, and explore complex problems that would have been insurmountable in the past. From drug discovery to climate science and beyond, AI is reshaping the way science is done. As technology continues to improve, the partnership between humans and AI will only grow stronger, accelerating the pace of discovery and unlocking new possibilities for the future. So, whether you're a researcher or just someone curious about the world, the age of AI-powered science is here, and it's only going to get more exciting!

9.5 Emerging Trends and Future Applications

Welcome to the thrilling final frontier of AI agents—where the future isn't just coming, it's already knocking at the door, ready to blow your mind. You know that sense you get when you're about to experience something groundbreaking, like when your favorite sci-fi movie just gets a whole new level of cool tech? Well, get ready, because we're on the brink of some pretty incredible things with AI agents. From autonomous vehicles to smart cities to AI-driven creativity, the future of AI agents is one where the impossible becomes possible, and the pace of innovation is quicker than ever.

So, what can we expect? First off, AI agents aren't just going to be sitting quietly in the background; they're going to be taking a leading role in shaping everything around us. We're talking about next-level personalization, virtual worlds so real you won't want to leave them, and smarter-than-ever systems that learn and adapt, often before you even realize what's happening. These emerging trends will make us rethink what technology can actually do—and how it'll redefine everything from our daily lives to the very fabric of society. Buckle up, because the future of AI agents isn't just about efficiency—it's about creating a whole new world of possibilities.

The Rise of Autonomous Systems

The first trend we're seeing is the massive rise of autonomous systems. AI agents are no longer just your assistant that helps you answer emails or suggests your next Netflix binge (though, let's be honest, it's also great at that). The future is all about self-driving cars, delivery drones, and robotic assistants that think on their feet (or wheels). These autonomous systems rely heavily on AI agents to make decisions in real-time based on their environment. As these agents improve in sophistication, we'll be seeing more and more applications in areas like transportation, logistics, and even public safety.

For example, self-driving cars are probably the most high-profile AI agents out there right now. These cars use an array of sensors and AI-driven decision-making processes to navigate the world. But the future of autonomous vehicles goes beyond just cars. We're talking autonomous trucks, buses, and even flying taxis that could change the way we think about travel, cities, and our daily commute. In fact, these agents will soon become so advanced that they will seamlessly integrate with infrastructure, like traffic lights and smart roads, creating a hyper-efficient transportation ecosystem.

AI Agents in Smart Cities

Speaking of smart infrastructure, smart cities are a huge emerging trend that will rely on AI agents to make our urban environments more efficient, livable, and sustainable. Smart cities use AI agents to monitor traffic, control energy usage, improve public services, and even ensure public safety. For instance, AI-driven systems could optimize street lighting to save energy or adjust traffic flow based on real-time data to reduce congestion. These systems will also play a crucial role in sustainable development, helping cities reduce their carbon footprint by intelligently managing resources like water and electricity.

AI agents in smart homes will also continue to evolve, becoming even more intuitive and integrated with our daily lives. We're talking about personal assistants that not only turn on the lights and play music but also learn your habits and anticipate your needs, such as adjusting the thermostat or ordering groceries when you're running low. Eventually, we'll see AI agents move beyond isolated home automation and into smart communities where entire neighborhoods, offices, and public spaces are interconnected, making life smoother and more energy-efficient.

The Future of Creativity: AI-Powered Art and Entertainment

Now, this one's fun: AI-driven creativity. It's not just about algorithms doing calculations or robots replacing factory workers anymore. AI agents are now starting to dabble in the world of art, music, literature, and more. And no, we're not talking about something as basic as using AI to enhance images or write basic articles (though it does a great job at that too). We're talking about AI that can compose music, write novels, and even generate visually stunning artwork. The AI art community is growing, and there are already some truly mind-blowing examples of AI-created masterpieces.

In entertainment, AI agents are being used to enhance user experiences. Personalized recommendations have already evolved beyond just movie suggestions—soon, AI will create entirely personalized TV shows, music playlists, and game narratives tailored specifically to you. AI agents will also become more involved in content creation for video games, where they'll generate increasingly sophisticated environments and plots, pushing the boundaries of immersive worlds. Picture a game world where the storyline changes and adapts based on how you play, with an AI agent acting as a dynamic storyteller. The line between interactive entertainment and reality is blurring.

The Role of AI in Healthcare

In the healthcare sector, AI agents are continuing to make waves in areas like diagnosis, drug discovery, and patient care. AI agents have already demonstrated their ability to detect cancerous tumors, predict patient outcomes, and suggest personalized treatment plans. The future of healthcare, however, lies in even more personalized medicine where AI will analyze your genetic makeup, lifestyle, and medical history to offer recommendations that are truly tailored to you. This will significantly improve the quality of care and treatment efficacy.

One fascinating application on the horizon is the idea of AI-driven health companions. These agents will not only track your health in real-time but also help in managing chronic diseases, suggesting lifestyle changes, and even predicting potential health risks before they become critical. The goal? Making healthcare more proactive rather than reactive.

AI Agents and Ethics: A New Frontier

As AI agents become increasingly autonomous and integrated into our lives, the issue of AI ethics will undoubtedly become more pressing. How do we ensure that these agents make ethical decisions? Will we be able to trust them? The rise of AI will require a deep dive into responsible AI development, ensuring that these agents are not just powerful but also fair and transparent.

We may also need to address the impact of AI on jobs and society. As AI agents take on more tasks, there will be an increasing need for reskilling workers to adapt to the new landscape. But don't worry—the future isn't all doom and gloom. While some jobs might be automated, new roles and industries will arise, and people will continue to be essential in steering AI toward creating positive impacts.

The Road Ahead

As we look to the future, the potential for AI agents seems limitless. From self-driving vehicles to smarter cities, and from personalized healthcare to AI-powered art, we're only scratching the surface of what these agents can do. As these agents become more sophisticated, they'll play an increasingly crucial role in solving some of the world's most pressing challenges, from climate change to healthcare access.

The key will be finding the right balance between innovation and ethics, making sure these intelligent systems are developed and deployed responsibly. The future of AI agents is exciting and full of possibilities, but how we shape that future will ultimately be in our hands. So, buckle up, because the next few decades are going to be one heck of a ride!

Chapter 10: The Future of AI Agents

Ah, the future. That mysterious time when robots might do your laundry and your taxes. But it's not all chrome and laser beams—this chapter explores the real challenges, the ethical dilemmas, and the high-stakes questions of trust, transparency, and collaboration with our artificially intelligent coworkers.

This final chapter addresses the future direction of AI agent development. We examine the differences between general and narrow AI, explore ethical and legal implications of intelligent systems, and analyze the evolving nature of human-agent collaboration. Additional discussion centers on transparency, explainability, and the technical and societal challenges that lie ahead.

10.1 General AI vs. Narrow AI in Agent Design

AI is one of those buzzwords that gets tossed around everywhere, and in the vast sea of artificial intelligence, two major concepts stand out like the alpha predators in the ocean: General AI and Narrow AI. These two types of AI agents are like two sides of a coin— one is all about versatility and ambition, while the other is focused, efficient, and sometimes a bit stubborn. So, what's the difference between them, and how does this relate to agent design? Let's dive into it, shall we?

The Basics of Narrow AI

First off, let's talk about Narrow AI (sometimes called Weak AI—which sounds a bit harsh, don't you think?). Narrow AI is the practical, workhorse AI that does specific tasks really well, but don't expect it to hold a conversation or, you know, think for itself. It's the AI agent that powers everything from your voice assistants to the self-checkout kiosk at your local grocery store. These agents excel in one area: solving a specific problem. They're like the world's best specialist who knows everything about one topic, but ask them to step out of their lane, and they'll be as lost as a dog in a library.

For instance, a Narrow AI agent might be really good at detecting fraudulent transactions in a bank system, but if you ask it to bake you a cake or play a game of chess, well… it'll probably just stare back at you. These agents don't have any understanding beyond their set parameters, and their decision-making is solely driven by the data they've been trained on. Think of Narrow AI as a specialized tool—very effective in its niche but no Swiss Army knife.

General AI: The Dreamer's AI

Now, on the other hand, there's General AI (or Strong AI—more like an overachiever, right?). This is the stuff of sci-fi movies and the AI equivalent of a Swiss Army knife, able to do anything and everything. General AI isn't just good at one task; it has the potential to understand and learn any task. It would have the ability to perform a variety of tasks just like a human—think of it as the Jack of all trades of the AI world. Want it to play chess? Done. Want it to write a novel? No problem. Need it to predict the weather? Sure thing. General AI can learn, reason, adapt, and apply knowledge across a wide range of fields.

In agent design, this type of AI agent would be built with a complex system of cognitive models—allowing it to process information, reason, and make decisions across different domains. It's the kind of AI we all dream about (and maybe a little bit fear), capable of performing tasks in any environment and solving novel problems. But here's the kicker—we haven't quite achieved General AI yet. We're still stuck in the world of Narrow AI (which, let's be real, is pretty cool, too).

Key Differences in Agent Design

Now, you might be wondering, "Okay, but what does all this mean for designing AI agents?" Well, the answer lies in how these two types of AI are designed and implemented. Narrow AI agents are typically designed with specific, limited architectures. They're programmed to perform specific tasks, and their decision-making processes are defined within those boundaries. The AI's knowledge base and learning methods are targeted for solving particular problems efficiently and effectively.

In contrast, General AI agents would need a whole different approach to their architecture. Their systems would have to be far more complex—able to reason, generalize knowledge, and adapt to a variety of tasks. They would rely on advanced learning techniques, such as transfer learning and meta-learning, to absorb knowledge across different fields. The challenge with designing a General AI agent is not only creating a system that can handle a broad scope of tasks, but also ensuring that it can integrate new information in real-time, much like how humans can switch between tasks effortlessly.

In practical terms, for most businesses and applications today, Narrow AI is where the action is. It's much easier to design and deploy agents that are hyper-specialized for a specific task. Whether it's a virtual assistant, a medical diagnostic tool, or an AI-powered chatbot, these agents are designed to do one thing really well, and they do it efficiently.

The Road to General AI

While General AI might sound like a futuristic dream, the road to creating such an agent is full of obstacles. We still don't fully understand human cognition, and thus, we're not sure how to replicate it in machines. Even the most cutting-edge AI researchers are just beginning to scratch the surface of consciousness, reasoning, and understanding in machines.

Moreover, developing General AI brings up major ethical concerns—for example, how do we ensure these agents act in the best interest of humanity? Would they make decisions that align with human values? And how do we prevent them from doing things that could harm us? These questions are just the tip of the iceberg, and they're at the forefront of discussions in the AI community.

Where Do We Go From Here?

While we're still far from creating true General AI, the cool thing is that Narrow AI is advancing at lightning speed. In the next few years, we'll see even more sophisticated specialized agents that can perform tasks in highly complex and dynamic environments. These AI agents will continue to evolve, and hybrid systems—those combining narrow agents with more flexible, generalized models—could take us one step closer to General AI.

But for now, when designing AI agents, we're stuck in the world of Narrow AI, and that's perfectly fine. For many applications, Narrow AI is exactly what we need. It's fast, efficient, and solves specific problems. The key takeaway here is that Narrow AI is already revolutionizing industries, from healthcare to finance to entertainment, and it will continue to do so for the foreseeable future. So, while the dream of General AI might keep us up at night (in a good way), don't sleep on the power of Narrow AI—it's got plenty of tricks up its sleeve.

And who knows? Maybe one day, we'll wake up to a world where General AI agents are as common as your morning coffee. Until then, though, let's enjoy the magic and possibilities that Narrow AI continues to bring to the table.

10.2 Ethical and Legal Implications

If AI agents were superheroes (and let's be honest, they might just be), we'd all be standing around in awe of their superpowers—the ability to analyze massive datasets in the blink of an eye, make complex decisions, and predict the future (kind of like a fortune teller, but much cooler and data-driven). But like any superhero, AI agents come with a set of responsibilities. With great power comes great responsibility, right? Well, when it comes to ethical and legal implications, AI agents may not just be doing the good stuff. They could also be putting us in tricky situations that we need to navigate carefully.

Imagine this: you've got a self-driving car powered by an AI agent, cruising down the road at top speed. It encounters a dilemma—a situation where it has to decide between swerving to avoid a pedestrian and crashing into a guardrail. What happens then? The car doesn't have human intuition, but it does have algorithms, and those algorithms are going to make that life-or-death decision based on the data they've been trained on. Now, where do we draw the line between ethics and legality when it comes to the decisions that AI agents make? And what happens when something goes wrong?

The Ethical Dilemma: Right vs. Wrong in AI Decisions

The first major issue in the ethical landscape of AI is the concept of decision-making—especially when it comes to making life-or-death decisions, like in autonomous vehicles or medical AI agents. For instance, in the self-driving car scenario, the agent has to make a decision about who to "save" in a potential crash. This is often referred to as the trolley problem in ethical discussions. Do you prioritize the life of the pedestrian, the car's passenger, or maybe even the greater good of society? The issue isn't as simple as choosing the "least harmful" outcome—it's about how we program AI agents to think in these high-stakes situations.

But even outside these high-pressure situations, AI systems are being used in ways that challenge traditional ethical frameworks. Consider an AI system designed to evaluate job applicants. Should the system favor candidates based on their resume keywords or their ability to think critically and creatively? And how do we ensure that the system doesn't perpetuate bias? If we don't program it carefully, it could unintentionally reproduce and amplify existing discriminatory biases, such as those based on race, gender, or socioeconomic status.

The ethical implications here go beyond the technology itself. It's about who decides what's right or wrong, and how we ensure fairness and transparency in those decisions. When AI agents are making decisions that affect people's lives, we need to ensure that these decisions are ethical, just, and aligned with human values.

Legal Concerns: Who's Responsible?

If you thought the ethical dilemma was tough to untangle, brace yourself—because legal implications are like the ultimate maze. When an AI agent causes harm, whether it's an accident, a mistake, or a system malfunction, the question becomes: who's responsible? Is it the developer who created the AI agent? Is it the company that deployed it? Or is it the AI itself, and if so, can we even hold an AI accountable?

Let's say an autonomous delivery drone drops a package on someone's head. The person sues. Who's at fault? Is it the developer who wrote the code for the drone's flight path? The company that owns the drone? Or, in a more dystopian future, could the AI be held responsible? While the idea of AI being "punished" sounds a bit like something straight out of a sci-fi movie, the reality is that legal frameworks are still catching up with the rise of AI agents. Right now, the law tends to hold humans accountable for AI agents' actions, but as AI becomes more autonomous, there's a growing need to define liability and accountability in AI-related incidents.

Furthermore, the question of data privacy is an ongoing legal issue when it comes to AI agents. These systems rely on massive amounts of data, often personal data, to function. How do we ensure that AI agents aren't violating privacy laws or misusing sensitive information? The General Data Protection Regulation (GDPR) in Europe is a good example of an effort to set rules around data collection, but these rules are still being tested in the context of rapidly evolving technologies. And with laws varying from country to country, it's a real headache for companies deploying AI agents globally.

Ensuring Fairness and Accountability in AI Development

One of the biggest challenges in developing ethical and legal AI systems is ensuring fairness and accountability. A huge part of the solution lies in ensuring that AI agents are not just blindly performing tasks based on their programming, but that they are transparent and auditable. If a decision made by an AI agent is challenged, there should be a way to trace how that decision was made. Transparency in decision-making processes is key to maintaining public trust.

Another important aspect is the idea of accountability frameworks. We need to ensure that the people who develop, deploy, and use AI systems are held responsible for their consequences. This means establishing legal standards that outline acceptable practices for AI development, deployment, and oversight. This also requires creating policies that enforce non-discrimination, data privacy, and user safety while minimizing the potential for harm. But here's the catch: AI development is moving fast, and the law? Well, it's trying to keep up, but it's usually a few steps behind.

Moving Forward: Ethics, Law, and AI Alignment

As we move forward into a world where AI agents are becoming more powerful and autonomous, we need to seriously reconsider how we approach both the ethical and legal implications of AI. We're standing on the edge of a new frontier where AI systems will have more influence over our lives—deciding who gets hired, how resources are allocated, and even who lives or dies in some situations.

The good news is that many researchers, companies, and governments are already working on frameworks to address these issues. Ethical guidelines and legal standards will likely evolve alongside AI development to ensure that these agents serve humanity in the best way possible. But for now, it's crucial that we proceed with caution, thinking not just about what AI can do, but what it should do.

So, the next time you interact with an AI agent—whether it's a chatbot, a smart assistant, or a self-driving car—remember that its actions are guided by algorithms created by humans, and those algorithms are influenced by our own values, biases, and ethics. The question is not just "What can AI do for us?" but also, "What should we let AI do for us?" The responsibility lies in our hands to guide these agents to a future where they don't just make life easier, but also better and fairer for everyone.

10.3 Human-Agent Collaboration

Picture this: you've got a coffee machine that knows exactly when you're running low on coffee beans, a virtual assistant that schedules your appointments while predicting when you'll need a break, and an AI-powered car that gets you to your destination while jamming to your favorite playlist. Sounds pretty awesome, right? But here's the twist: all of these tasks are not being done entirely by the machines. Humans and AI agents are working hand in hand, complementing each other's strengths and weaknesses in a way that's creating a future where collaboration—not competition—is the key to success. Welcome to the world of Human-Agent Collaboration, where you, the human, get to be the brains behind the operation, and your AI agent is the brawn.

In this dynamic partnership, you're not just barking orders at your virtual assistant or letting the machine do its thing without a second thought. No, no, no. In fact, the most successful collaborations happen when humans and AI agents communicate, learn from each other, and play to their strengths. Think of it like this: you bring creativity, empathy, and judgment to the table, and your AI agent brings raw computational power, endless data processing, and the ability to execute tasks without breaking a sweat. Together, you're a powerhouse. But just like any good team, human-agent collaboration requires balance. You wouldn't want your assistant doing all the thinking for you, just as you wouldn't want to handle all the tedious tasks without any help. It's about teamwork.

The Synergy Between Humans and AI Agents

The magic happens when humans and AI agents combine their respective advantages in ways that lead to better decision-making, increased productivity, and ultimately, better outcomes. Think of a doctor working with an AI-powered diagnostic system. The doctor brings expertise, experience, and empathy to the interaction, making critical decisions based on a patient's unique needs. Meanwhile, the AI agent can analyze massive amounts of medical data, spot patterns, and offer suggestions that the human doctor might have missed. This collaboration can significantly improve diagnosis accuracy, reduce human error, and help the doctor make more informed decisions.

AI agents excel in areas where humans might struggle. Take repetitive, time-consuming tasks, for example. AI can crunch data faster than a human could even dream of, making it the perfect assistant for tasks like sorting through mountains of customer feedback, tracking inventory levels, or running simulations for financial modeling. In contrast, humans are much better at tasks that require empathy, creativity, and complex decision-making—skills that AI hasn't mastered (yet!). So, when AI takes over the grunt work, humans can focus on what they do best: thinking outside the box, building relationships, and solving complex problems.

This dynamic is already being explored across a variety of industries, from healthcare to finance to customer service. AI agents are being used to assist rather than replace humans, enabling professionals to work more efficiently while adding more value to their role. And here's the kicker: it's not just a one-way street. The collaboration isn't about humans dictating to machines; it's about the two learning from each other and evolving together. AI systems can be taught by humans, but they can also help humans learn, making us more efficient and informed than ever before.

Human-AI Collaboration in the Workplace

Let's bring this back down to earth and think about the workplace. As more businesses adopt AI agents to help with everything from project management to customer service, the role of human workers is shifting. Instead of spending hours combing through spreadsheets or responding to routine queries, workers are now freed up to focus on higher-level tasks that require judgment, creativity, and interpersonal skills. AI becomes the assistant—the hard worker behind the scenes—but humans are still at the helm, making the big decisions and overseeing the work.

Take, for example, AI-powered chatbots in customer service. These bots can answer common questions, troubleshoot issues, and even make product recommendations, all while learning from previous interactions. But when it comes to complex or sensitive situations—like an upset customer, a billing dispute, or a tricky technical issue—it's still up to the human agent to step in and provide that personal touch. The AI is helping to triage issues, streamline processes, and ensure that humans aren't bogged down by menial tasks, but when it's time for a human to step in, the AI knows when to hand over the reins.

This concept of human-AI collaboration is becoming a central pillar in business strategies because it enables companies to leverage the best of both worlds. AI can process large datasets, find trends, and automate repetitive tasks with unmatched precision. But the decision-making that requires ethical considerations, emotional intelligence, and creative problem-solving still belongs to the humans. This partnership is leading to a future where workers are more focused, productive, and creative, while AI agents handle the heavy lifting.

Collaboration in Critical Sectors

In industries like healthcare, AI-powered tools are being used to analyze medical images, predict patient outcomes, and recommend treatment options. While these tools can process more data in seconds than a human doctor could in a lifetime, doctors still use their experience and intuition to make the final call. The patient's well-being depends on the collaboration between human expertise and AI precision. Similarly, in fields like finance, AI agents can scan thousands of financial reports and news articles to spot market trends. But it's the human financial advisor who combines that analysis with understanding of the client's needs, risk tolerance, and financial goals to make the best investment decisions.

This isn't about replacing jobs or eradicating human roles—it's about enhancing them. AI doesn't have emotions, ethical values, or the ability to think creatively in the way that humans do, and for now, we're still the ones who bring the critical thinking and emotional intelligence to the table. The secret to success in human-agent collaboration is understanding that these agents are tools—they're there to augment, assist, and amplify human capabilities, not to replace them entirely.

The Future: AI and Humans as a Power Duo

As we look to the future, the potential for human-agent collaboration is boundless. With advancements in AI, we'll see even more specialized agents designed to assist in creative endeavors, complex decision-making, and human-centric tasks. From AI writing assistants that help authors brainstorm ideas to AI in the arts that assists with composition, humans and machines are going to team up in ways that were once the stuff of science fiction. AI won't just be a tool; it'll be an integral part of every creative and professional process.

In conclusion, human-agent collaboration isn't just a buzzword or a trend—it's the future of work, creativity, and problem-solving. While AI agents are good at what they do, it's humans who will keep things grounded, making sure that our values, ethics, and goals are at the forefront of every decision. By collaborating with AI, we unlock the potential for humans to focus on what really matters, leaving the boring and repetitive tasks to our trusty AI assistants. And who knows? Maybe one day, we'll look back and realize that the key to achieving our greatest successes was never about AI agents doing the work alone—it was about humans and machines working together as one, each bringing their own unique strengths to the table.

So, let's embrace it. Together, we'll get things done better, faster, and smarter. Because when humans and AI work in harmony, there's nothing we can't accomplish.

10.4 Transparency, Explainability, and Trust

Alright, imagine you're getting ready to make an important decision in your life—maybe it's choosing between two career paths, or deciding what pizza toppings to order (I know, tough decisions). Now, what if someone came along and told you, "Here's the right choice," without offering any explanation as to why or how they came to that conclusion? You'd probably feel a little uneasy, right? It's like buying a car based solely on someone's recommendation without knowing the specs or understanding how it works. You'd want to know why that car is the best option, how it works, and what makes it the right choice for you. Well, when it comes to AI agents, this need for understanding and clarity is even more critical.

Transparency, explainability, and trust are the cornerstones of ensuring that we don't just use AI agents like magic boxes that spit out answers without ever knowing how they reached those conclusions. Think of it this way: AI agents are like your very smart but incredibly mysterious friend who's great at solving problems but doesn't always tell you how they do it. Over time, this friend could become a little less trustworthy if you're never let in on the secret sauce behind their genius. When we start introducing AI agents into serious decision-making processes—whether it's in healthcare, finance, or even when giving feedback about your pizza preferences—we need to be able to trust that these agents aren't pulling answers out of thin air or relying on mysterious "black box" algorithms. We need to understand how and why the agent made its decision.

Transparency: The Foundation of Trust

Transparency is the first step to building trust. In the world of AI, transparency means that we, as users, should have clear insights into how an AI system works. This includes understanding the data that the AI has been trained on, the algorithms it uses, and the decision-making process it follows. If an AI agent is making life-altering decisions—say, a medical diagnosis or a loan approval—you'd expect to know why it made the decision it did, wouldn't you? Transparency gives us the reassurance that the AI isn't just pulling results out of nowhere but is instead following a well-defined process based on concrete data and reasoning.

To make this a bit more real, let's imagine an AI system used in a loan approval process. Instead of just giving you a "yes" or "no" answer when you apply for a loan, the system should explain, "You didn't qualify because your credit score didn't meet the threshold, and your monthly debt-to-income ratio was too high." This breakdown isn't just nice to have; it's essential for building trust. If an AI agent can be transparent in how it operates, we can better understand and, ultimately, trust its decisions. It's like when a friend explains their reasoning behind a decision—having that clarity helps us feel more comfortable.

Explainability: Making Complex Decisions Understandable

Transparency is a great first step, but let's be honest, we also need explainability. Transparency without explainability is like being told, "The car runs on electricity," without ever being told what that actually means or how it works. Explainability takes transparency one step further. It's not enough just to know that an AI system works on a certain set of data and algorithms. We need the system to clearly explain its reasoning in a way that is understandable to the human users.

Think about it: you're sitting in front of a decision-making AI, and it's telling you something complex like, "This investment will likely return 10% in the next 5 years based on historical market trends." But how did it come to that number? What data did it look at? What assumptions are in play? Explainability is about giving humans a chance to understand the logic behind the AI's decision-making process. It's like opening the hood of a car and showing how everything works, so the user knows exactly what's going on under the surface.

For example, imagine you're working with an AI-powered recruitment tool that sorts through job applications. Instead of simply saying, "This candidate is a match," the tool could explain: "This candidate has experience in the required skillset, a degree in the relevant field, and scored highly in personality assessments that align with the company's values." With this level of explainability, you're no longer in the dark about why a decision was made, and you can make more informed choices based on that explanation.

Trust: Building Confidence in AI Decisions

Now, here's the million-dollar question: How do we trust AI? It's a good question because, let's face it, trusting something that's machine-based can feel like trying to trust a vending machine not to give you the wrong snack (we've all been there). Trust in AI comes from understanding the reasoning behind its decisions (thanks, transparency and explainability), knowing that its creators are being ethical in their programming, and having confidence that it isn't simply reinforcing biases or making mistakes.

One of the most important aspects of trust-building is ensuring that the AI is fair. You don't want an AI system making decisions based on flawed data, or worse, biased data. Imagine an AI that's been trained on biased hiring data and ends up favoring one gender or race over others. Trust would be broken in an instant. For this reason, developers need to make sure that AI systems are constantly audited, that they undergo regular checks for fairness, and that they are transparent about how they process sensitive information. This constant diligence helps build the public trust in AI, ensuring that we're not putting our faith in a system that could let us down when it matters most.

Another component of trust is reliability. If an AI agent is making crucial decisions, like diagnosing a health condition or recommending a life-changing financial investment, it needs to be consistent and reliable. You can't trust a system that gives you contradictory answers on the same problem. Ensuring that AI agents consistently deliver accurate, well-supported outcomes is key to gaining trust.

The Road to Trust: Human-AI Collaboration

At the end of the day, the trust between humans and AI is a two-way street. For AI agents to be fully accepted and integrated into our lives, they must demonstrate that they can be trusted to act in our best interest. But trust doesn't come from AI systems alone; we need to trust in the people who design and deploy these systems, too. If the humans behind the AI are transparent about how the agents work, explain their decisions clearly, and prioritize ethical practices, then trust will grow naturally over time.

As AI systems become more integrated into industries like healthcare, finance, and customer service, the need for trust will only grow stronger. In these critical areas, we need to be confident that the AI is working for us, not against us. Transparency, explainability, and trust will be essential not just for building systems that work well, but also for ensuring that AI technology can be used safely and ethically.

So, the next time you interact with an AI agent, remember that trust is a delicate thing. It's built on clarity, explainability, and the knowledge that the system you're using has your best interests at heart. When transparency and explainability are embedded into AI systems, trust becomes not just a hope but a reality—a foundation that makes AI agents truly useful partners in our future.

10.5 The Road Ahead: Opportunities and Challenges

Alright, if you've stuck with me this far, then you're probably as pumped about AI agents as I am. But hold onto your seat, because the road ahead isn't all sunshine and rainbows. Yes, AI agents are incredible, but like any technology, they come with their fair share of opportunities and challenges. Think of it like setting off on an epic road trip: you've got a cool destination in mind (the future of AI), but there will be some bumps, detours, and occasional roadblocks along the way. So, what does the future hold for AI agents? Well, let me take you for a little spin.

First off, let's talk about the opportunities. AI agents are poised to revolutionize almost every industry out there. Whether it's in healthcare, finance, education, or robotics, AI agents are the golden ticket to improving efficiency, making smarter decisions, and even tackling some of humanity's biggest challenges, like climate change or disease prediction. Imagine a world where your health monitoring device doesn't just track your steps but can detect early signs of a health issue before you even realize it. That's the potential of AI agents—solving problems we never thought possible. But it's not all about solving grand challenges. These agents are also set to reshape the everyday—think autonomous cars, smart homes that actually know what you need before you do, and AI-powered assistants that will handle your life's admin so you can focus on what really matters (like binge-watching your favorite show without feeling guilty).

But—and this is a big "but"—along with these opportunities come some serious challenges. First, let's talk about the ethical implications. AI agents are only as good as the data they are fed, and if that data is biased or flawed, well, you've got a big problem. What happens if an AI system used in a hiring process or criminal justice system perpetuates existing biases? Trust in AI would take a nosedive, and rightly so. This means we need to ensure that AI systems are not only effective but fair and unbiased. Developers, policymakers, and users alike need to be vigilant about the ethics of AI, ensuring these systems are used responsibly and equitably.

Next up, transparency and explainability—two words that should be tattooed on every AI developer's forehead. We've talked about how crucial it is to know how and why an AI agent makes its decisions. But getting AI systems to be fully transparent is no easy task. Some of the more sophisticated algorithms, especially in deep learning, can sometimes operate in ways that are so complex they become near-impossible to explain. This presents a serious challenge to trust. After all, how can we trust something if we don't understand it? And let's be real, we're not all ready to just blindly accept decisions from a machine. This is one of the key areas of focus moving forward.

Another hurdle is human-agent collaboration. AI agents are fantastic at processing vast amounts of data and providing insights, but they're not perfect (yet). We're still in the early stages of integrating AI agents into our daily lives, and the human element is just as important. Can AI agents work seamlessly with humans, complementing our decision-making instead of taking over entirely? Or will we have to constantly babysit them to ensure they don't make a mess? Building AI systems that can collaborate effectively with humans is not only crucial for their success but also for their acceptance in society. We're talking about a future where you and your AI assistant aren't adversaries but partners in achieving goals.

And let's not forget the technical challenges. Developing AI agents that can handle real-time decision-making in ever-changing environments is no small feat. These agents need to adapt to new situations, update their knowledge, and make informed choices without running into issues like data overload or algorithmic bottlenecks. The scalability of AI agents is another issue we'll need to address. As these systems grow more complex and are deployed across more industries, the infrastructure behind them needs to evolve to keep up.

Finally, the regulatory landscape will play a huge role in shaping the future of AI agents. We're seeing a growing push for AI regulations and guidelines, but they are still lagging behind the technology. How will we ensure that AI agents are used safely? What are the rules for data privacy? Who's responsible if an AI system makes a mistake? Governments and organizations around the world need to establish frameworks to address these questions, but they also need to strike the right balance between innovation and regulation. Too much red tape could stifle progress, but too little could lead to dangerous consequences.

So, while the road ahead is full of promise, there are plenty of potholes and speed bumps to navigate. The future of AI agents isn't a smooth ride from point A to point B. It's more like a fast-paced adventure, filled with exciting opportunities, tricky challenges, and a need for all of us to stay on our toes. The good news? We're all part of this journey. As AI continues to evolve, so do we. And as long as we keep our eyes on the road, ask the tough questions, and build with responsibility, the future of AI agents looks like it could be one heck of a ride. So buckle up, folks. The best is yet to come.

Well, here we are. If you've made it to the end of this book, first of all—congratulations. You now officially know more about AI agents than 99% of people who've ever tried to get their smart speaker to "just play the song I'm thinking of." You've navigated the wild world of rational agents, environmental chaos, architecture debates, planning puzzles, and a few ethically-questionable decision trees. You've learned how agents sense, think, act, plan, and sometimes, spectacularly fail in the most human ways possible. In short: you get it. And that's a big deal.

This book was never about just memorizing terms or diagrams (though if you did, gold star). It was about pulling back the curtain on the digital minds quietly shaping the future around us. Whether you're here to build, research, teach, or just be able to argue at dinner parties about what "intelligent" really means, I hope you've had as much fun reading as I had writing it. And if you've laughed, questioned, or side-eyed an AI system a little differently because of this—mission accomplished.

Now, let me be clear: this isn't the end. Oh no, this is just the first step in the *Mastering AI Agents: From Theory to Deployment series*. If you're itching to roll up your sleeves and build something, flip right over to the next book—**Building AI Agents with Python: A Hands-on Guide**. That's where things get practical, messy, and extremely satisfying. Then we head into the deep end with **Reinforcement Learning for AI Agents**, where agents learn by doing, failing, and eventually thriving (kinda like me learning to bake).

Still with me? Good, because we're only getting started:

In Multi-Agent Systems, we explore what happens when agents have to work together (chaos, mostly, but also brilliance).

AI Agents in the Real World shows how theory hits the ground running—in smart homes, cities, and businesses.

AI Agents for Automation tackles everything from chatbots that almost pass the Turing test to assistants that might one day run your calendar better than you ever could.

AI Agents in Finance, Healthcare, Cybersecurity, and Robotics each dive into domain-specific uses, where agents aren't just helping—they're leading innovation.

To everyone who's joined me on this journey, whether you're a student, a developer, a curious soul, or someone who just really likes robots: thank you. You gave this book a purpose. I'm genuinely honored you chose to learn with me. If you found clarity, insight, or just a few laughs, then we're doing something right. AI may be about machines—but writing this? That was all heart.

Now go. Keep learning. Keep building. And maybe—just maybe—build an agent that finally understands what you meant when you said, "Set a reminder for dinner, not Denver."

See you in the next book.